About Island Press

Since 1984, the nonprofit organization Island Press has been stimulating, shaping, and communicating ideas that are essential for solving environmental problems worldwide. With more than 1,000 titles in print and some 30 new releases each year, we are the nation's leading publisher on environmental issues. We identify innovative thinkers and emerging trends in the environmental field. We work with world-renowned experts and authors to develop cross-disciplinary solutions to environmental challenges.

Island Press designs and executes educational campaigns, in conjunction with our authors, to communicate their critical messages in print, in person, and online using the latest technologies, innovative programs, and the media. Our goal is to reach targeted audiences—scientists, policy makers, environmental advocates, urban planners, the media, and concerned citizens—with information that can be used to create the framework for long-term ecological health and human well-being.

Island Press gratefully acknowledges major support from The Bobolink Foundation, Caldera Foundation, The Curtis and Edith Munson Foundation, The Forrest C. and Frances H. Lattner Foundation, The JPB Foundation, The Kresge Foundation, The Summit Charitable Foundation, Inc., and many other generous organizations and individuals.

The opinions expressed in this book are those of the author(s) and do not necessarily reflect the views of our supporters.

City Forward

City Forward

HOW INNOVATION DISTRICTS CAN EMBRACE RISK AND STRENGTHEN COMMUNITY

Matt Enstice with Mike Gluck

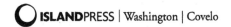

ISLANDPRESS | Washington | Covelo

Library of Congress Control Number: 2021951368

All Island Press books are printed on environmentally responsible materials.

Manufactured in the United States of America
10 9 8 7 6 5 4 3 2 1

Keywords: Anchor institution; Buffalo; collaboration; community engagement; development guidelines; diversity; economic prosperity; education; equity; inclusive growth; innovation district; leadership; renewable energy; resilience; social design; sustainability; transportation

Contents

Foreword

In the continued craze over innovation and the pursuit of place-based innovation, what continues to be undervalued, if not overlooked entirely, is the necessity of reflective leadership. Harnessing the soft and hard assets of anchor institutions (such as universities and medical institutions) and innovation districts to help achieve more equitable communities demands leadership.

Without leadership, large institutions and companies will never come together to pursue collaborative approaches to research and development, they will not create a competitiveness agenda that values the sharing of ideas and assets, and they will fail to translate their strengths into lifelong opportunities for adjacent communities.

Leadership is a characteristic I described in the Brookings research paper "The Rise of Innovation Districts: A New Geography of Innovation in America." Districts are an emerging geography of innovation found predominantly in cities and urbanizing areas that strive to strengthen their competitiveness through a "collaborate to compete" model. The research argued how and why the collapse-back of innovation into cities was a growing phenomenon due to the convergence of multiple economic, demographic, and cultural trends. Collectively, these trends revalued high-quality, compact places where people, including talented workers, exchange highly complex knowledge and work to advance collaborative forms of innovation in close quarters, easing the friction of time and travel. Although all this sounds highly theoretical, the paper documented the rise of a new kind of local and collaborative leader ambitious to do more.

In this book, Matt Enstice gives us a view of what reflective leadership looks like and feels like and shows us how difficult it can be. Matt and his colleagues at the Buffalo Niagara Medical Campus (BNMC) understand how the development of buildings is only the physical manifestation of mission-driven, deeply needed ambitions. For Matt and a growing chorus of people in Buffalo and around the world—from many different backgrounds and experiences—a core mission is the process of rebalancing long-standing inequities that limit the true potential of people of color, economically disadvantaged people, women, people experiencing homelessness, and many other groups.

Emerging primarily in the cores of cities, innovation districts in the United States are often adjacent to neighborhoods characterized by high levels of poverty and low levels of educational attainment. The physical proximity of asset-rich institutions to communities often at or below the poverty line is a painful contrast that organizations, such as BNMC, fight to correct.

The challenging but important work of balancing innovation and inclusive growth is, and should be, a core mission of anchor institutions and innovation districts around the globe. In nearly every corner of the world, disparities related to race, ethnicity, religion, gender, and other factors can be found in any aspect of regional economies, including education, workforce training, access to good jobs and career advancement, pay, leadership opportunities, startup activity, and access to capital. As a result, regional economic growth is restricted and, more crucially, economic mobility and access to prosperity for marginalized groups in the United States and globally are severely limited. The data on persistent intergenerational poverty among Black people in the United States, for example, establish clear linkages to residential and school segregation policies.

This focus on equity also helps explain why you will not find a chapter here that is devoted to a traditional definition of city building. Instead, this book provides a powerful and accessible narrative about what it means to rebuild and reimagine community. In his effort to braid together commonly divided worlds, Matt paints a picture of unbalanced power, painful memories, and mistakes but, most importantly, the tenacity to keep trying until there is some form of change.

I close by sharing how this book reminds me of why I founded, and now lead, The Global Institute on Innovation Districts, a new not-for-profit organization dedicated to the growth of innovation districts worldwide. This ambition was not borne out of a desire to keep the status quo; it was sparked by the ambition to alter the dangerous growth trajectory our societies have created. The painful inequalities and systemic racism (something that I and far too many others experience) that continue to increase, the sprawling development patterns and polluting practices that undercut the ability to save our planet, and the myriad health challenges—from cancer to diabetes to the inability to access healthcare—that continue to plague our communities are all high on the daunting list of challenges we face.

Anchor institutions and innovation districts, though not a solution for all things, if designed by leaders like Matt, can become our world's place-based problem solvers. From what I see, feel, and have come to understand, as I traverse the globe to support the growth of innovation districts, geographies aligned and equipped to be problem solvers are our only path forward.

Julie Wagner
President and Founder of The Global Institute on Innovation Districts

Preface

When we started the Buffalo Niagara Medical Campus in the early 2000s, there was a lot of friction and tension between our anchor institutions and the surrounding neighborhoods. In fact, the city's common council president told me, "Don't you dare try to build anything east of Michigan Avenue." Michigan Avenue marked the border between the campus and a historic Black neighborhood, so I guess he was trying to protect the neighborhood. But I was young and naïve and determined, so I walked across Michigan Avenue and met with the pastor of the city's largest Black church to see how we could work together.

One of the first things he asked was why our master plan for the campus didn't include any plans for his community. It was funny, really—we had elected officials telling us to leave the neighborhood alone, even when the people who lived there wanted to be included, and we wanted to work with them.

We ended up partnering with that pastor and his church to get a grant from the Robert Wood Johnson Foundation. The foundation team told us that we convinced them as soon as the pastor, Amy Schmit (our first executive hire), and I walked into the room together for our presentation. By showing up together, we proved that we were actually working together, not just talking about it.

That was a huge turning point for me, because it showed that you shouldn't just listen to the status quo and do what's always been done. You need to put yourself out there and really work to build those partnerships—even if they seem unlikely when you start.

We've learned countless lessons since then, and we're still learning today. My hope is that you can learn from our successes—and our mistakes.

✿ ✿ ✿

Cities can't do what cities used to do.

Limited resources, population shifts, and other challenges such as COVID-19 make it difficult to sustain basic services, let alone do more.

So how do we undertake one of the most essential missions of our time and create more equitable cities? How do we ensure that more people have more access to high-quality healthcare, affordable housing, reliable transportation, a good education, and sustainable economic opportunities?

In this book, you'll learn what has worked—and what hasn't—in cities across the country, with real-life lessons that highlight the extraordinary successes (and failures) of communities nationwide. If you've ever said, "I wish I knew that before I started," this book is for you. Consider this your practical manual for how anchor institutions and innovation districts can become agents for urban change—from crafting a vision to managing the inevitable challenges along the way. Simply put, it's a playbook for you to follow as you work to foster innovation, advance equity, and build a stronger, more resilient community.

✿ ✿ ✿

Our focus will be on anchor institutions and innovation districts.

Anchors are typically large, well-established, nonprofit (or not-for-profit) organizations, including educational, medical, and cultural institutions. Given their size, stability, and deep roots in the community, anchors and anchor districts are powerful. In fact, anchors are the largest employers in two thirds of America's cities; anchors own the infrastructure, manage the resources, and have the political capital needed to drive change.

Innovation districts add private industry to the mix, creating environments "where leading-edge anchor institutions and companies cluster and connect with start-ups, business incubators, and accelerators."[1] As public and private institutions join forces, these innovation districts attract investment, spark development, and wield considerable influence.

⚙ ⚙ ⚙

When it comes to creating more equitable communities, anchors and innovation districts can pick up where cities leave off and play a distinct, invaluable role for society. One way for anchors and innovators to promote equity is by working individually (or with other anchors and innovators) toward solutions that benefit the entire community. Think of an art museum offering free admission, or an innovation district that sets employment targets for underrepresented groups. This "Anchors and Innovators Alone" model can help create more equitable communities, in which everyone has fair access to opportunities. But this model often leads to top-down decision making, with anchors and innovation districts telling the community what the residents need.

In consulting with communities from around the United States and working to build a more equitable city over the past twenty years, we've found a more effective way: the "Anchors and Innovators Plus" model.[2]

"Anchors and Innovators Plus" simply means that the anchors and innovation districts intentionally engage with others—including community groups, governments, nonprofit organizations, and private businesses—who share the commitment to create more equitable communities. Anchors and innovators can (and often should) still lead community-wide efforts, but they should be very cautious about doing it alone.

☼ ☼ ☼

Welcome to Buffalo, New York. Once a national punchline, Buffalo is now on the front line of communities that are creating more equitable cities.

Why Buffalo? Perhaps it starts with our nickname: the City of Good Neighbors, the official slogan introduced by mayor Thomas L. Holling back in 1940. Here, we go above and beyond for each other, whether we're helping a neighbor shovel their sidewalk after a snowstorm or welcoming thousands of refugees as one of the leading cities for resettlement in the United States.

So it's no surprise that when the Buffalo Niagara Medical Campus (BNMC) was founded in 2001, one of the questions our leaders kept asking was, "How do we help people?"

Instilling that culture of empathy was one of the most important things, especially at the beginning. That focus drove everything we did—and still drives us today. It's not just about what's best for the BNMC. It's about what's best for Buffalo, period. (That said, we weren't really thinking about equity from the start. We were just trying to get things done on the campus, and we knew from tours of other cities that partnering with the community and having them on board was often the deciding factor for whether a project succeeded or failed.)

I didn't realize it at the time, but this collaborative approach would quickly make the BNMC a trailblazer in what we now call social design: an intentional, transformative approach to creating a more resilient future—and, in our case, a more equitable city.

"What makes BNMC unique as an anchor is that instead of defining its objectives on the basis of its own institutional needs and what its operations can contribute, the organization has created a vision and goals based on the needs of the communities around it," wrote business strategist and social design expert Cheryl Heller in her book *The Intergalactic Design Guide: Harnessing the Creative Potential of Social Design.* "It invites neighbors into the conversation, asking them what's important to them and then incorporating that into the plan," added Heller, who coined the phrase "MutualCity" to define the BNMC's social design–driven approach.

Applied consistently over the past twenty-plus years, social design has helped Buffalo achieve extraordinary results. The BNMC is often recognized as a leading model in the United States in terms of both economic development ($1.7 billion in projects announced or under construction at one time) and social change. Our MutualCity outcomes include everything from urban farms and bikeshare programs to clean energy and job training initiatives. We are a founding member of the Global Institute on Innovation Districts and a member of the National League of Cities' exclusive City Innovation System program. Elected officials, urban planners, and community leaders from across the country seek our help in addressing inequality in their communities.

There's still more work to do, of course—across the country and in our own backyard. Buffalo is one of the worst regions in the country in terms of racial segregation, poverty rates for children, and other key measures. And we've certainly made mistakes along the way. But we believe that we're on the right path—learning and growing, teaching and sharing, and using the principles of social design to advance equity.

If we can do it in Buffalo, you can do it anywhere. Every community has the potential to be the City of Good Neighbors.

⚙ ⚙ ⚙

Regardless of what you call it—social design, anchors and innovators plus, or MutualCity—bringing people together isn't easy. It's a messy process (with an emphasis on process) that takes longer and inevitably ruffles some feathers. But engaging the community helps eliminate unintentional blind spots, raises awareness about the unique opportunities (and privileges) afforded to influential institutions, and serves as a self-fulfilling reminder of the need for a diverse group of decision makers. Communities that follow the model are rewarded with real, community-supported progress toward creating a more equitable city.

Here are just a few examples of how the "Anchors and Innovators Plus" model works in communities large and small, old and new, coast to coast:

A top-performing school for underserved students in St. Louis: In a city that made national headlines after the killing of Michael Brown and subsequent Ferguson riots, anchor institutions worked directly with the school district to address racial tensions and structural inequity. Together, the anchors and school system founded a STEM magnet school that attracts underserved students and achieves extraordinary results, including test scores that rank first across the entire public school system.

Healthy returns (and missed opportunities) in Indianapolis: The Indianapolis Cultural Trail—a collaboration between half a dozen cultural anchors, a community foundation, and the city—landed on the coveted *New York Times* Best Places to Go list, contributed to a billion-dollar increase in assessed property value, increased revenues for businesses along the path, and attracts hundreds of thousands of users each year (including recreational walkers and cyclists, as well as commuters). However, the question remains: What could have been done—and what can be done in the future—to address unintended consequences of the trail, including "exorbitant property value increases and displacement of residents" in working-class neighborhoods?[3]

Solar power for low-income residents in Buffalo: As the city's tech-hungry hospitals grew, they worked with one of the world's largest energy companies (National Grid) on a plan that offered opportunities for everyone, including a more flexible and resilient microgrid for hospitals and free solar panels for low-income residents in adjacent neighborhoods. The resulting initiatives addressed outdated infrastructure ("Thomas Edison himself touched the wires in your system," joked one executive), enabled unprecedented growth on campus, and helped some of the city's poorest homeowners save up to 25 percent on their electricity bills.

A new innovation district makes a commitment in Phoenix: Launched in 2018, the PHX Core innovation district was founded with a clear focus on creating a more equitable community. Their strategic plan outlines their support for a more walkable city, light rail expansion, inclusion-focused programming, and stronger engagement across community groups. The plan was informed in part by a benchmarking visit to Buffalo, during which nearly two dozen leaders from Phoenix toured Buffalo's medical campus and learned firsthand about the opportunities to transform a city through the "Anchors and Innovators Plus" model.

⚙ ⚙ ⚙

Cities can't do it alone.

But as Rosanne Haggerty, president of Community Solutions, said in a speech celebrating the fiftieth anniversary of New York City's zoning laws, we must find ways to "create better lives for all who live here." (You'll read more about Rosanne in chapter 8.)

It can be done.

We're here to help show you how.

Acknowledgments

As an English major in college, I sometimes fantasized about writing a book. Little did I realize how rewarding and enriching the experience would be, in large part thanks to the incredible group of people who have made it possible.

The team at the Buffalo Niagara Medical Campus includes some of the most talented, driven people I've known, including Adriana Viverette, Elizabeth Machnica, Harmony Griffin, Jamie Hamann-Burney, Kyria Stephens, Marla Guarino, Mark McGovern, Patrick Kielty, Patrick Kilcullen, Sam Marrazzo, Sharese Golding, Trent Howell, Linda Limina, Zach Cottrell, and Janine Gordon. This book is a testament to their work and to the many contributions of all of our past employees. I am proud to call them my colleagues and friends. I especially thank Kari Bonaro and Maria Scully Morreale for the countless hours they spent helping to shape this book and bring it to fruition, and Dayle Cotter for keeping everyone on track and working efficiently. I couldn't have done it without you.

The Buffalo Niagara Medical Campus member institutions support our work, keep us moving in the right direction and provide endless contributions to the community.

Our board of directors guides us in building a more equitable community. I am indebted to all of our current and past board members for their efforts. I would also like to acknowledge everyone on our "Better Together" group of religious leaders, as well as those involved with our work councils. The leaders and staff at The Global Institute on Innovation Districts have consistently provided support and thought leadership. President Julie Wagner helped connect us with equity-focused leaders around the world and was gracious enough to write the foreword for this book. Cheryl Heller is a brilliant designer who developed the MutualCity framework that shaped much of our thinking.

Many elected officials and their staffs have helped support our goals to build a stronger community through the years. These people dedicated to public service include U.S. senator Charles Schumer, U.S. representative Brian Higgins, and NYS governor Kathy Hochul. NYS senator Timothy Kennedy and assemblymember Crystal Peoples-Stokes have been huge advocates for Buffalo. Erie County executive Mark Poloncarz, and former Buffalo mayor Anthony Masiello have provided critical support throughout the years. I am also indebted to many former elected officials, including Paul Tokasz, Dale Volker, Hillary Clinton, Thomas Reynolds, Jack Quinn, Jr., and Louise Slaughter.

Thank you to everyone we interviewed while writing this book, including Dennis Elsenbeck, Jeff Epstein, Sam Fiorello, David Gamble, Kären Haley, Janice Henderson, Curt Hess, Carlos Jaramillo, Lillian Kuri, Thomas Osha, Baiju Shah, Lucy Kerman, Dennis Lower, Laura Oggeri, Chris Ronayne, Stephanie Simeon, Marilyn Swartz-Lloyd, Paulina Villa, and Tom Yardley. Your examples and insights were extraordinarily helpful.

Although I had the honor of writing about many of the people who have encouraged our work, I simply did not have room in this book to mention everyone who played a significant role in the growth of the Medical Campus and the ongoing development of the City of Buffalo.

Those who aren't specifically noted include Ruth Bryant, Juweria Dahir, George DeTitta, Sir Peter Gershon, Bob Glenning, Jane Griffin, David Hohn, Marlon Kerner, Rudy Wynter, Alex Krieger, Ken Kurtz, James Magavern, Bill Maguire, Herman Mogavero, Jim Madej, John Pettigrew, David Parker, Rick Reinhard, Cynthia Schwartz, TNH Nation, James Wadsworth, and Jon and Heather Williams.

I'm thankful to Ed Saltzberg for introducing me to Julie Marshall at Island Press. If you have the chance to work with Julie, Heather Boyer, and the team at Island Press, I recommend it. Specifically, I would like to recognize our extraordinary editor and tireless advocate, Courtney Lix, who has done an incredible job of transforming this book from a simple idea into the text you're reading today.

Throughout this process, I worked closely with Mike Gluck, who researched topics, conducted interviews, developed the structure for the book, and helped write much of the content. Additional thanks to Johanna Hess, Casey Reinhardt, Elizabeth Im, and Yasmin A. McClinton.

I know I am not supposed to do this, however I have to highlight selfless leaders who have been great mentors and supporters for me personally as the BNMC has grown—Tom Beecher, Tony Martino, Bill Joyce, Jerry Jacobs, Dave Zebro, Jim Biltekoff, and Ted Walsh.

On a personal note, I want to thank my parents, siblings, and mother-in-law, my brothers- and sisters-in-law, my nieces and nephews, and friends; you all rock! I am extraordinarily grateful for my wife, Jessica, and our kids, Molly and Tommy. Your patience, understanding, and love keep me going, every day. You are the foundation that keeps me real.

Finally, for everyone working to make their community a better place, this book is for you. Thanks for your passion, dedication, and commitment to building a more equitable world.

All proceeds from this book will be used to further diversity, inclusion, and equity-related efforts throughout our community.

Equality and equity are not the same. Credit: A collaboration between the Center for Story-Based Strategy and the Interaction Institute for Social Change. https://www.story basedstrategy.org/the4thbox and http://interactioninstitute.org/

Introduction

I wrote this book because I firmly believe that anchor institutions and innovation districts can lead the way in building more equitable cities. But before we go further in talking about how anchor institutions and innovation districts can close the equity gap, let's agree on a few key premises.

First of all, inequity exists. Some people undeniably have more access to more resources than others.

Next, equity is good for society. As former president Barack Obama stated, "In this country, of all countries, a person's zip code shouldn't decide their destiny."[1] (A quick aside: although "equity" and "equal" both come from the Latin *aequus*, they mean different things. In an equal system, everyone is treated identically. In an equitable system, everyone is treated fairly. If you give a homeless person and a millionaire each $100, you're treating them equally but not equitably.)

In building an equitable society, we must recognize the value of diversity and inclusiveness. Diversity makes our cities richer—economically and culturally. It makes our entire community stronger, and it benefits everyone. But having a diverse society isn't enough; we must strive for inclusiveness, in which all members of a community can participate and benefit.

Finally, let's agree that cities should be at the forefront of our conversations about equity. Cities are where most Americans live. They're often the site of the greatest disparities in inequality, and they represent the greatest potential to build a more equitable society.

What Is Equity, and Who Is It For?

When we talk about creating more equitable cities, it's important to recognize the many different *types* of inequalities and inequities. Access to healthcare. Access to education. The digital divide. Disparities in income. From air pollution to affordable housing, inequity is as ubiquitous as the sidewalks in our cities—and the results can be fatal. In the United States, for example, your life expectancy is ten years shorter if you're poor than if you're rich.[2] The short- and long-term consequences of inequity affect individuals, families, neighborhoods, and entire communities.

We must also think about *who* is affected by these inequities. Many communities allocate considerable resources toward helping their poorest residents, addressing racial inequities, integrating immigrants and refugees, and providing access to residents who are disabled. Although these are noble efforts, many other groups face inequities small and large on a daily basis. Is your community safe for everyone, regardless of their gender identity? Can seniors and children easily navigate your city? How are you serving people who are mentally impaired? Think about these and other groups in your community and how you can address their needs.

Many equity-related issues are intertwined. In some cases, the *types* of inequities are interrelated; for example, poverty is linked to negative health outcomes, from mental illness to coronary heart disease. In other cases, certain *groups* may be disproportionately affected by specific inequities. For example, Black pedestrians "were struck and killed by drivers at a 82 percent higher rate than White, non-Hispanic Americans."[3]

Therefore, it's crucial that we think about equity in a holistic manner and attempt to uncover the root cause of inequities. In Buffalo (as in many cities across the United States), income inequality can be traced in part back to redlining of Black neighborhoods, which made it extraordinarily difficult for Black people to get mortgages and build wealth. Buffalo's Fruit Belt neighborhood and Masten District, both adjacent to the Buffalo Niagara Medical Campus, were two of these communities. Understanding some of the underlying reasons for income inequity helped us build trust with the community (a crucial step that we'll explore further in chapter 4) and create programs to help address inequity.

What Is an Anchor Institution?

An anchor institution is an institution that, like an actual anchor, typically stays in one place. An anchor institution is tied to the community, not only because of its physical presence but because it serves a distinct purpose for the people in that specific city. Traditional anchor institutions, also known simply as "anchors," include universities and hospitals ("eds and meds"), as well as museums, other cultural institutions, and foundations. Without anchor institutions, our cities would be much different places.

What Is an Anchor District?

An anchor district is an area that includes one or more anchor institutions. Sometimes called anchor collaboratives, these districts are typically defined by geographic boundaries and are usually in cities—often near neighborhoods facing high unemployment rates, poor health outcomes, and other signs of inequity, which is how many districts first become involved in equity-related efforts.

Organizations that choose to form an anchor district usually share a vision, a common purpose, or at least a specific logistical need such as parking. Most anchor districts include a core group of members, including the anchors as well as other sizable or influential organizations. Other businesses and organizations (such as restaurants and startup companies) are often located within an innovation district but may not be official members of the district.

What Is an Innovation District?

In some ways, "innovation district" is just a more modern way to say "anchor district." In fact, if we were starting today we would probably call ourselves the Buffalo Niagara Innovation District instead of the Buffalo Niagara Medical Campus.

Depending on how you count them, there are easily more than one hundred innovation districts around the globe as I write this book, and there may very well be dozens (if not hundreds) more by the time you read this. Spain's 22@ District in Barcelona is typically cited as one of the first innovation districts in the world; in the United States, that honor often goes to Kendall Square in Cambridge, Massachusetts (ironic, given that it was once called "Nowhere Square"). Many of these innovation districts have evolved organically. In some cases, there was a single precipitating event; in Philadelphia, for example, the University City District was sparked by tragedy after a University of Pennsylvania biochemist was fatally stabbed walking home with his fiancée. In cities such as Las Vegas and Detroit, corporations have led carefully planned efforts to create innovation districts.

The most commonly cited definition of an innovation district is typically from Julie Wagner and Bruce Katz's seminal article "The Rise of Innovation Districts," in which they described innovation districts as areas where anchors and businesses "cluster and connect with startups, business incubators and accelerators" in an area that is "physically compact, transit-accessible, and technically-wired" and includes "mixed-use housing, office, and retail."[4]

There isn't a formal definition for what constitutes an innovation district, which explains why some so-called innovation districts seem to be little more than marketing and branding exercises. For the purposes of this book, I'll define an innovation district as one that includes anchors (including universities, hospitals, and cultural institutions), is located in a city, and may include housing, office, and retail space.

What an Innovation District Isn't

An innovation district is not a large geographic region known for innovation. Silicon Valley is not an innovation district. Neither is New York City.

An innovation *center* is typically a building or two, home to startups or perhaps a particularly forward-thinking company. Although an innovation center can be part of an innovation district, it does not, by itself, constitute one.

Research parks and science parks (terms used to describe districts typically centered around research-oriented universities and institutions) aren't necessarily innovation districts, but they certainly share some of the same characteristics. Many of the traditional science and research parks are located on or near suburban college campuses, not in urban environments, although we are pleased to see some of the nation's leading universities "un-anchoring" and moving into cities.[5]

An Evolving Role for Anchors and Innovation Districts

Founded in 1751, Pennsylvania Hospital in Philadelphia is the first hospital in the United States, making it one of the oldest anchor institutions in the country. For most of its early existence, the hospital—like most anchor institutions—focused on its core mission, including taking care of patients and educating future physicians.

Today, Pennsylvania Hospital is one of thirty-one shareholders in a leading innovation district—a district that is fueling its growth through partnerships with a global co-working group, a real estate developer, and a real estate investment trust.[6]

As the times have changed, so have anchor institutions and innovation districts. In the beginning, they focused primarily inward, on their own goals and milestones. Hospitals kept communities healthy. Museums provided unique cultural experiences. Universities attracted and educated students from around the world. For decades, these outcomes were good enough, at least for many anchor institution and community leaders.

But good enough, as is often the case, wasn't good for everyone. Although the anchor institutions' efforts affected the community, the primary motivation wasn't necessarily to better the community as a whole. A hospital might cure a sick patient but would probably have little interest in whether that patient's family had nutritious food to eat or whether their children attended a good school. For years, most of these organizations weren't approaching the community holistically, nor were they thinking in terms of advancing equity.

Some signs of progress came throughout the twentieth century, as anchors and innovation districts became increasingly aware of their role in the community and made more efforts to hire local vendors and employees and, to varying extents, involve the community in their decision making. These changes came about for a variety of reasons. Society was becoming more aware of growing inequity, and they often put pressure on anchors and innovation districts to do more beyond their walls and their traditional areas of focus. And organizations, to their credit, recognized the connections between their institutions and the community, often because of the anchors' location in the heart of underserved communities.

Now, in the early twenty-first century, anchors and innovation districts clearly recognize that they must do more than provide jobs. They understand the impact—both positive (more employment opportunities) and negative (increasing housing prices)—that their growth can have on the surrounding neighborhoods. They are taking on roles traditionally served by governments, from providing grants for neighborhood gardens to taking the lead on creating a regional mobility hub, to name just a few of the things we've done here in Buffalo. And, especially in larger cities, they are bringing in partners to help manage real estate development and provide funding (we'll explore some of the ramifications of these trends in the Conclusion). Of course, with more development and more funding comes an even greater need to ensure that these initiatives are actually helping people in marginalized communities.

The Impact of Anchor Institutions and Innovation Districts

"Austin Medical Innovation District Would Generate $800M, 2,800 New Jobs, Study Finds."[7] That's a typical headline about innovation districts, focused on the fact that they are typically top economic drivers for a city and region thanks to employment, construction, and other factors. A growing innovation district also spurs development in nearby neighborhoods; in Buffalo, of all the projects issued permits by City Hall over the course of a decade, approximately 30 percent (by value) occurred within a mile of our campus.

Beyond the financial impact, innovation districts play a unique role in facilitating collaboration, especially between institutions that do not typically work together or, in some cases, are outright competitors.

Bringing together universities, hospitals, governments, communities, and other groups creates a forum where these organizations can solve problems and share ideas, as we'll discuss in much more detail in later chapters. Through these collaborations, innovation districts often take on practical initiatives that individual institutions can't do as efficiently and effectively on their own, such as district-wide safety and parking initiatives. An innovation district can also help make a region more attractive for investment, if that's your goal. Think about this: Can equity be a differentiator for the people and companies you're trying to attract and retain?

Beyond the Numbers: Impact on Equity

In the past, we've often defined successful anchor institutions as ones that are doing well financially. They're able to fulfill their mission, grow, and hire people in the community—and by doing so, advance economic prosperity and strengthen the surrounding neighborhoods. But perhaps these aren't the only metrics we should be using to measure success. If our goal is for anchor institutions and innovation districts to promote equity, we must look at their impact through an equity lens.

There are certainly ways to promote equity through development, such as having a certain percentage of a construction budget that must go to minority- or women-owned enterprises. Beyond jobs, anchors and innovation districts can model best practices for equitable communities—for example, by building walkable infrastructure. Anchors and innovation districts can work with community groups to influence city-wide development guidelines (such as green space requirements for new buildings) and can provide critical support to developers who are committed to the community. In Buffalo, we offer our medical campus as a test site for renewable energy projects developed throughout the region. Innovation districts can also champion socially minded causes that individual institutions can't or won't take on. We've found that most organizations want to have a positive social impact but may lack the resources or political capital to lead the charge, especially if it's not part of their core capabilities. That's why our innovation district has introduced programs such as EforAll and Eforever (which you'll read about in chapter 10) and helped fund and launch a bikeshare program now in its fifth successful year of serving the city.

Why take the lead on equity? We've already discussed the moral reasoning for an equity-focused approach. If you're looking for more tangible justification, consider that anchor institutions and innovation districts are often funded in large part through public funds; in my experience, it's foolish (at best) to ignore the needs of the public when you're taking their money. In addition, working with communities to build a more equitable city not only can help you reach your stated goals; it can (and often does) help you raise the bar in terms of what you can achieve. There's an African proverb on the wall of our boardroom: "If you want to go fast, go alone. If you want to go far, go together."

Finding Our Purpose

When we formed the Buffalo Niagara Medical Campus, the needs of the surrounding neighborhoods were not initially at the forefront. Equity was not a primary consideration. In the beginning, we simply recognized that projects in other cities often stalled because of community opposition. So we decided that we would have nothing to hide. We would include everyone from the beginning.

But there's a difference between having nothing to hide and actively working toward a more equitable society. It was Alex Krieger, an urban planner who came to Buffalo early on in our planning stages, who said we have to be more inclusive and engage the community. We listened to him, and in retrospect, it was the best decision we could have made. Thanks to his initial push, we now have countless examples of successful community-driven collaborations, many of which are covered in later chapters.

Yet there was a moment, more recently than I'd like to admit, when I was walking through the Innovation Center on the Buffalo Niagara Medical Campus and realized that almost everyone looked like me—only twenty years younger and with a lot more hair. We may have been including people, but we weren't doing enough to intentionally advance equity.

So we decided to take the next step. We developed our MutualCity philosophy, which has proven to be a more effective approach in promoting change. (MutualCity is a term coined by social design expert Cheryl Heller to describe our process, but it really doesn't matter if you call it "inclusive innovation" or "common destiny" or "MutualCity," as long as you're doing it.[8]) Through MutualCity, we began to focus more deliberately on social design and on finding win–win opportunities that would benefit the community as well as the innovation district. A few years later, the MutualCity philosophy led us to start the EforAll program in Buffalo, bringing a more intentional, accessible approach to entrepreneurship. A year after the launch of EforAll, we published this book as a natural extension of our ongoing learning process, giving us the opportunity to inspire others and let people learn from our mistakes.

I'm telling you about our process and journey because it was—and still is—a process and a journey. It's never finished. In fact, throughout the years a clear pattern has emerged: Every new thing we do often reveals something else that we're *not* doing. That's partly a reflection on the nature of our work; equity won't be "solved" in my lifetime. But as you read this book, I hope you'll recognize that some of the greatest successes in advancing equity are the result of ongoing, intentional, and deliberate work. That's why I encourage you to keep asking, every day, what else you should be doing. It's never too late. As the saying goes, the best time to plant a tree was twenty years ago; the second-best time is now.

The Limits of Anchors and Innovation Districts

Of course, there are limits to what anchor institutions and innovation districts can do. As our local newspaper wrote, the Buffalo Niagara Medical Campus "isn't a panacea. It won't on its own solve all of the region's big health care challenges, eliminate poverty in nearby neighborhoods, or suddenly make Buffalo the medical version of Silicon Valley."[9]

Anchors and innovation districts can't pass legislation. They can't levy taxes. And they can't build infrastructure outside their borders. In all these cases, they're reliant on government. For example, in Buffalo we want to make our district more walkable, which means adding signage in and around intersections. Simply installing stop signs to improve pedestrian safety on our campus requires approval from City Hall.

Geographically, anchors and innovation districts are often limited by their borders. They can transform their immediate streetscape, perhaps even influence adjacent neighborhoods, but don't typically produce a city-wide impact, especially in larger metro areas.

Finally, anchors and innovation districts may find themselves caught in the middle when it comes to balancing the demands of their customers (or shareholders) with the needs of their communities. For innovation districts with a large corporate presence, this becomes even more of a precarious balancing act (although, as we'll discuss at length, a more inclusive process can lead to win–win scenarios).

Because anchors and innovation districts can't single-handedly achieve more equitable communities, it's important to collaborate with other organizations that work in different areas, with different populations, or can offer additional expertise. For example, one of our nonprofit partners helped us design green infrastructure to minimize sewer overflows and water pollution (our sewer system is tied into the Niagara River, home to world-famous Niagara Falls). Creating and maintaining clean waterways isn't part of our core mission, but we can't have an equitable community without equitable access to drinkable, fishable water. This same nonprofit, Buffalo Niagara Waterkeeper, has also led efforts to remediate the local Buffalo River (featured in the *New York Times* 52 Places to Go), including the removal of one million cubic yards of contaminated sediment.[10]

Of course, you certainly don't need anchor institutions or an innovation district to promote equity. Long before innovation districts even existed, religious institutions were helping the poor. Today, there are countless nonprofit agencies, community development groups, governments, and other organizations working to create more equitable cities.

Beware of Unintended Consequences

Even when anchor institutions and innovation districts are focused on serving the community, their success can unintentionally exacerbate inequities. Boston's Kendall Square, the self-proclaimed "most innovative square mile on the planet," is notorious for its traffic.[11] Gridlock isn't just bad for research ("you can't cure cancer stuck in traffic"); it lowers the air quality, reduces pedestrian safety, and ties up valuable real estate for parking.[12]

We've faced similar issues in Buffalo, especially as our innovation district has grown (including adding 300 percent more companies in one three-year period). Residents from neighboring communities have used petitions and protests to draw attention to a range of issues, from lack of parking and gentrification to rising rents and the changing fabric of the neighborhood. And we've worked closely with neighborhoods—both proactively and reactively—to address everyone's concerns. We worked with the City of Buffalo and Kaleida Health to ensure that funding from the sale of a parking garage went directly into supporting infrastructure improvements in the Fruit Belt. We created a microgrant program to fund resident-led projects in the surrounding communities. We hosted in-depth leadership training for neighborhood stakeholders in conjunction with the University at Buffalo, Roswell Park Comprehensive Cancer Center, and Leadership Buffalo. But even the best solutions aren't necessarily best for everyone. For example, one of our anchor institutions recently built a new clinical science center at the edge of campus. The building won a prestigious architecture award, and the anchor took steps throughout the process to mitigate the impact of the building on the community (including building on a vacant lot to avoid displacement), but the reality is that the residents across the street suddenly had an eleven-story tower looming over their backyards. That wasn't the anchor institution's intent, of course. But intent doesn't matter if you're the one living in the shadows (literally) of a growing innovation district. Throughout this book, I've tried to be upfront about the fact that there's an inherent power dynamic between anchor institutions (and innovation districts) and the communities they serve. As an innovation district, we continuously strive to eliminate this dynamic—or at least mitigate it and adjust for it—but the fact is that large institutions have "power" in the traditional sense when it comes to control of land, capital, networks, and other resources.

Measuring Equity

How do you measure equity in your community? In some cases, you'll find existing tools to measure various factors, such as the Municipal Equality Index, which measures LGBTQ+ inclusion based on public information and government feedback about a city's laws, services, public positions, and other factors.[13] Cities can use these data to raise their scores; for example, the city of Grand Rapids, Michigan, improved their score in part by adding an LGBTQ+ liaison to the police department. Numerous organizations, including the U.S. Census Bureau, provide data that measure racial and ethnic diversity. In other instances, you may have to create your own measurement system. Of course, with any type of scoring mechanism, be mindful of the potential for harm, especially when people outside marginalized communities are the ones doing the measuring. People often have biases that influence the way data are collected, and the resulting scores can lead to inequitable actions and outcomes; remember that redlining happened when a federal agency graded neighborhoods based partly on their racial makeup.

Either way, consider two points: First of all, measuring equity won't be as quick or easy as reporting on jobs, construction, and other factors with more tangible outcomes. It takes time for everyone to agree on what to measure and how to measure it. Second, you probably won't have the data to perfectly prove that your efforts are improving equity, so think about what you can measure instead. In Buffalo, for example, we don't have the data to link health outcomes throughout the city directly to our healthy eating efforts, but we know that community gardens promote healthy lifestyles, so we continue to support the gardens.

Equity is an exceptionally complex topic, and even today it's not always at the forefront (for example, the top-ranked urban policy program in the country has a course about race, ethnicity, class, and gender—as an elective).[14] I recognize that this is a very brief overview of equity; if you'd like to learn more, I encourage you to view the resource list at the end of this book.

COVID-19, Black Lives Matter, and Equity

I can't end this introduction without talking about some of the most pivotal events of the decade: the COVID-19 pandemic and the Black Lives Matter movement.

Surely we'll be dealing with the full consequences and reverberations of COVID-19 for years to come. I'm proud of the fact that anchor institutions and innovation districts here and around the world helped conduct clinical trials of vaccines, provided emergency funding for small businesses, and found ways to supply healthcare workers with much-needed ventilators and personal protective equipment. But COVID-19 undoubtedly had a disproportionate effect on equity throughout the community. Older people, people of color, Indigenous communities, people experiencing homelessness, and those incarcerated all suffered higher mortality rates. Millions of low-paid "essential workers" commuted to jobs that were suddenly life-threatening, given the deadly airborne virus. A "she-cession" was attributed in part to women staying home to care for children whose schools and day care centers closed. Anti-Asian hate crimes spiked nearly 150 percent.[15] The list goes on and on. Many of these inequities existed long before the emergence of COVID-19, but the virus certainly exacerbated and magnified them.

The Black Lives Matter movement—fueled by the deaths of George Floyd, Breonna Taylor, and far too many others—inspired millions to march in the streets, protesting violence against Black people. This violence isn't new; we simply live in a time when more people are seeing and hearing about it, thanks in part to smartphone videos and social media. (Many drew parallels between the deaths of George Floyd and Emmett Till, a Black teenager murdered in 1955.) As the Black Lives Matter protesters grew stronger in number and voice, cities declared racism a public health crisis, police departments reviewed their training methods and explored more ways to partner with social workers, and more and more people learned about the continued impact of systemic racism.

Anchor institutions and innovation districts will continue to play a significant role in addressing inequities in healthcare and systemic racism, as we have for years. What's different now is that there are new inequities to address and that more people throughout society (not just people in marginalized communities) understand what we're doing and why we're doing it. The COVID-19 pandemic and Black Lives Matter movement have helped shine a much-needed spotlight on the inequities that persist in every community. It's clear that society in general is now increasingly aware that improving equity strengthens our communities.

How to Read This Book

This book is about how to promote equity rather than the exact steps you should take. The most effective tactics often differ between communities, and even within a community the best approach may change over time. As Cheryl Heller wrote, "The Process Is the Strategy."[16] The right process will lead you to the right actions.

To share the most effective processes, we've built this book around the lessons we've learned firsthand and from talking and working with anchor institutions and innovation districts around the country. Each chapter is focused on one key lesson, and the chapters are arranged in the order we think will be most useful, with lessons building on each other. That said, you can certainly skip around based on the specific issues you're dealing with at any time.

CHAPTER 1

Good Luck, It Will Never Happen

"Rat go home! Rat go home! Rat go home!"

That was the chant that greeted me as I walked up to a construction site on the Buffalo Niagara Medical Campus (BNMC).

The chant was coming from some union workers, who were upset because I had arranged for a nonunion crew to move some utility lines. The unions were calling me a "rat" for hiring nonunion workers. To emphasize their point, they had brought a huge inflatable rat to the job site.

Fortunately, it's not every day that I have to explain to my kids why people were calling me a rat all day long. But it's a story I remember every time I walk past that intersection.

Opposition: Part of the Process

When you've had some success, it's easy to forget about all the conflicts and obstacles you've faced (and continue to face) along the way. But when you're trying to build something—literally or metaphorically—learning how to handle criticism and manage conflict is one of the most important things you can do.

The truth is, we've had critics since the very beginning. In fact, when we were in the early stages of planning the BNMC, we invited one of the top community leaders to a meeting at a local club, where we enthusiastically shared our vision for the campus.

His advice couldn't have been more blunt. "Good luck," he said. "It will never happen."

Opposition is a natural part of building, growing, and running an anchor institution or innovation district. Even the most successful organizations deal with critics on a regular basis. In our case, much of the criticism we faced—especially in earlier years—was because we hadn't yet fully embraced social design and the MutualCity philosophy. Even though we were more collaborative with the community than similar organizations at the time, in retrospect we weren't as actively engaged as we could have been. We weren't as proactive and intentional in our efforts to promote equity. And, as a result, we weren't as effective in serving the community. The critics were right to complain.

You may not always see or hear about these battles, depending on how vocal the opposition is or how much the media choose to cover. But rest assured that even the organizations you admire the most are probably facing the same types of battles you are.

In fact, if there's a big project or program on our campus that *doesn't* have any apparent opposition, I start to ask, "Why not?"

Is the project or program truly good for everyone involved? Are the critics just being silent, waiting until later to voice their concerns? Do people who would be negatively affected even know that it's happening? If so, do they feel empowered to share their concerns? Do they have the opportunity to be heard? Just because you don't hear the critics doesn't mean they aren't out there.

At the BNMC, we certainly have our fair share of critics. We've been called out (as have many innovation districts) for promoting gentrification and for not doing enough for the surrounding communities. Some of this is in our control, and some isn't. As an innovation district, we can't stop gentrification. But we advocate for legislation that helps prevent it. We survey communities to get more information about what they need. And we work to mitigate its impact by helping people stay in their homes, including supporting organizations such as the Fruit Belt Community Land Trust, which promotes "development without displacement."[1]

We also recognize that the neighborhoods bordering the campus are distinct areas, each with its own unique demographics and needs. In the Fruit Belt neighborhood to our east, 83 percent of the people are Black; in Allentown to our west, 8 percent are Black.[2] Yet there are also similarities; the Fruit Belt and Allentown have nearly identical poverty rates. So when we're listening to our critics, we need to understand not only their concerns but also how they relate to that community—which is what will lead to an effective solution.

We can do better. We're not right all the time. Nobody is. But part of our commitment to equity and inclusiveness means that we don't shy away from criticism. When we saw that people who lived in the Fruit Belt couldn't park on their own streets because employees of our anchor institutions were parking there, we secured funding to study parking patterns, brought groups together, and identified solutions that would benefit the local residents. When we heard that our neighbors didn't have equitable access to nutritious foods despite all the development on the campus, we helped create the Moot Senior Community Center community garden to make fresh produce accessible to community residents, and we worked with the Massachusetts Avenue Project to set up a weekly mobile farmers' market. We're constantly inviting others to evaluate what we're doing, why we're doing it, and how we can do it differently to serve the community.

Not a Simple Fix

One of the reasons it can be so difficult to deal with opposition is that your opponents (and the systems they support) have been in place for years, if not decades. Most of the time, you're not going to change their minds overnight.

To keep perspective, I sometimes think about Niagara Falls, which is just a short drive from our campus. For centuries, the Falls have actually receded a few feet each year, as millions of gallons of water rush over the bedrock, slowly wearing it away. Of course, if you try to measure the change each day, it will be difficult (if not impossible) to see. But if the water keeps flowing and you come back in a year, you can clearly see progress. Persistence counts.

I've learned time and time again that advancing equity is a process. It's not something you can assign to a task force and accomplish in a year. The work is never-ending, and the issues are constantly changing. Some of this change happens slowly—for example, because of population shifts and changes in the demographic makeup of your community. Some of it happens rapidly, because of sudden factors such as COVID-19. Critics can pop up at any step along the way, which is why it's important to be flexible and able to adjust your plans, as we'll talk about more in the Conclusion.

Your Critic's Point of View

Understanding why people are opposed to your organization is an important step in dealing with critics. Perhaps the most obvious reason why people oppose you is that your plans aren't in their best interests. People who benefit from cheap labor, for example, will probably be hesitant to raise the minimum wage.

When you're facing a critic, ask yourself, "What threat does my plan pose to this person?" It could be tangible (lower profits), or it could be more vague (a threat to their identity). As we'll talk about in future chapters, it's important to really listen to people's objections and try to understand them, even if you don't agree with them.

When we were told, "Good luck, it will never happen," I don't think it's because our ideas were horrible. Instead, I think it's because the traditional leaders in town, including the one standing next to us, simply weren't open to change. They benefited from what one author calls the "entrenched power structures that are the source of comfort for some and oppression for others."[3] They had most of the power, so why would they endorse anything that would change that?

Not surprisingly, many objections come down to money. For example, cities are often focused on increasing the tax base. So if your goal is to turn 10 acres of land into affordable housing instead of luxury apartments, recognize that your goal is in conflict with one of the city's primary aims. Simply knowing your opponent's objection can be a useful starting point. For example, if the primary objection is financial, you can counter by showing how an equity-focused approach can help your city save money in the long term, perhaps by reducing the need for social services. One of our programs addressed the issue of urban food deserts by developing more healthy food options; we'll probably never know how much our community saved in hospital visits, sick days, and other costs, but I firmly believe that these types of programs pay for themselves many times over (in addition, of course, to being key steps in advancing equity). We are always looking for ways to demonstrate the impact of equity-focused solutions; as this book is being published, we are launching a new project to improve healthy habits (such as increased intake of fruits and vegetables and more physical activity) and then measure changes in healthcare use and other factors.

These equations won't always be easy. For example, autonomous vehicles will ideally reduce the number of accidents and lower air pollution, among other benefits for communities. However, cities may lose millions of dollars in parking fees and fines with the rise of self-driving cars.

Many innovation districts—including the BNMC—count on parking fees for a significant portion of their revenue. So how do I balance our need for revenue with the long-term benefits for our community?

We face these challenges every day, whether we're thinking about autonomous cars or affordable housing or countless other issues. In fact, when you're talking about equity, many disagreements come down to a similar standoff: on one side, a short-term view of one's own interests, versus a big-picture view of what's best for society, including unknown cost savings that you probably won't see for years.

One common reason for not engaging in equity-related work is "That's not what we do." Institutions tend to focus on their core missions, which can cause conflict when you're trying to get them to engage in equity-related initiatives. If you ask a hospital to commit time and money toward a program that promotes buying from local farmers, for example, they may be reluctant because it's not directly related to patient care. When we faced this challenge in Buffalo, we didn't start by trying to convince a healthcare system that it was the right thing for the community; instead, we showed leaders how it would benefit their business. When we demonstrated how buying local could help them meet sustainability goals, keep budgets in check, and improve patient satisfaction rates, it was easy for them to say yes. We weren't going to change the healthcare system's mission, but if we could frame our goals in terms of their needs, we could both come out ahead. (Even if people don't have a reason to oppose you, they may not have any incentive to support you, either. For example, most businesses are designed to make profits; very few have an explicit mission to improve society.)

Some people will be against you simply because they're unwilling or unable to take certain risks. For example, in one city, a major research university wanted to test autonomous vehicles within the innovation district, but the city government wouldn't allow it because of liability concerns. There was little (if any) reward for the city, compared to what they perceived as a high risk. The conflict came down to a disagreement about the amount of risk and who was willing to assume it. Perhaps similar conflicts could be resolved by quantifying the actual risk or by finding a way to transfer some or all of the risk from the city to the university.

Some of your most vocal critics will surely point to past failures as proof that you, too, are doomed. When I started working to establish the BNMC, there was a stack of old plans 3 feet tall. But just because the plans didn't gain traction ten years earlier doesn't mean they were a bad idea. If someone says, "We tried that already," ask why it didn't work then—and think about what's different now.

Emotion versus Facts

When you hear criticism, it's usually either a logical argument or an emotional argument. Understanding which type it is can help you process it and respond effectively.

Logical arguments are based on facts. They're typically more straightforward because you can determine whether the facts are true and discuss them accordingly. One of the common problems is that people confuse opinions with facts. "Your hospital isn't doing enough to help the community" is an opinion, not a fact. ("Your hospital provided only $50,000 in community-based services last year" is a fact.) Even when people do rely on facts, they're often basing their arguments on old data—often a prominent issue that got a lot of news coverage but has already been resolved. For example, three years after we were involved with (and helped resolve) a neighborhood-wide parking dispute, people still bring it up to me as an example of what we do wrong. If you're going to have a data-based discussion, make sure you have the most current data.

When it comes to understanding the source of conflict, you also have to consider the emotions behind the opposition. Some people are afraid of the unknown. Some people are angry that their world is changing.

Some people simply don't want equity. Emotions are often more powerful than logic, and understanding and acknowledging these powerful forces can help you get closer to a solution that everyone can agree to.

As you're facing opposition from various individuals and organizations, don't lose sight of the underlying, intangible obstacles to equity, such as systemic racism and gender discrimination. It's easy to get caught up in feuds and yell at an elected official or send a harshly worded email to a developer. But ask yourself whether you should be focused on the person or on the bigger issue.

If you've been doing this work for a while, you already know that society is becoming increasingly polarized—often with a negative impact on equity as "each group fends for itself above all others."[4] Of course, this polarization is exacerbated by social media platforms, which tend to reinforce our beliefs and further divide us rather than promote thoughtful discussion. So as you're dealing with critics, consider how much they just want to "win" rather than truly finding common ground. And recognize that some people will refuse to give in. When cities were forced to desegregate public pools, for example, some cities simply closed their pools rather than integrating them.

Identify, Focus, Embrace

Whenever we have critics, I try to do three things as quickly as possible: identify who the critics are, figure out who I need to work with, and then embrace them.

So how do you figure out which critics to work with? Obviously, if you're battling with someone who controls your funding or can block government approval, you'll want to pay close attention, especially if they're talking with the media. But in my experience, the loudest and brashest critics aren't really the most dangerous. It's the quiet critics you really have to watch out for—the ones who are silent in the beginning but try to block you after you've invested significant time and money into a project. In most cases, they aren't deliberately waiting to ambush you. These are the people who aren't accustomed to speaking out. They don't have power in the traditional sense. But they're powerful because they have something personally at stake.

A few miles from our medical campus is the Richardson Olmsted Campus, one of the country's largest historic preservation initiatives. Architect David Gamble, one of the urban designers behind the original 2003 master plan for the BNMC (while employed at lead firm Chan Krieger & Associates), also helped direct the Richardson Olmsted Campus master plan. In these endeavors, where tensions are high and community buy-in is essential, one of the first things the master plan team did was establish a community advisory group. (Robert Shibley, dean of the School of Architecture and Planning at the University at Buffalo, was an engagement specialist in both planning efforts and was instrumental in identifying community leaders for the groups.)

For the Richardson Olmsted project, the committee met monthly and was composed of people who "had the most at risk, and were also potentially critical of what was going to happen," says Gamble. Having these people at the table from the beginning allowed the team to "take the temperature" of stakeholders about the proposed plans and "vet the things that we were going to present to the broader public—and that then helped guard against potential misunderstandings about the project."

You're going to have to work to find these people. As we were first developing our innovation district, I spent months attending community meetings, just quietly listening, learning, and earning people's trust. Think about who will be affected most by your plans. Take a walk around the neighborhood. Talk with the corner shop owners. Keep an eye on social media. Their voices may be softer, but if you listen closely you'll hear them.

Thinking about your potential critics is a good exercise even in the initial brainstorming process for new projects. For example, if you need to expand, your first instinct shouldn't be to expand into a marginalized neighborhood simply because the residents there have been stripped of their political power and are therefore less likely to be vocal in their resistance. Having less opposition doesn't necessarily mean you're doing the right thing.

Getting Them on Your Side

So what do you do with the most vocal critics? Why not give them the biggest microphone? In Oklahoma City, the mayor made his strongest critic the head of the committee charged with reviewing a key task force.[5]

You may never quiet your critics completely by embracing them—nor should that be your goal. (As the former head of the University of Pennsylvania wrote, "Sure, many residents who used to rail against Penn are still screaming at us. But now that they are at the table, they do not shout quite as much or quite as loudly."[6]) But working with—not against—your critics is an invaluable opportunity for you to mitigate their impact, learn from them, and ultimately come out stronger, together.

Sometimes, it's even possible to convert critics into supporters. In Buffalo, the city's common council president, Jim Pitts, warned us not to expand the campus into the neighborhood he represented. So we asked him to serve on our board. It took a while, but this former foe became one of our staunchest supporters and even agreed to join our board.

Fortunately, we've also had many friends and supporters from the start. U.S. senators Charles Schumer and Hillary Rodham Clinton helped bring much-needed attention and resources—including $10 million in federal funding—to the campus. The Heron Foundation helped us create a business plan to manage our growth. Jeremy Jacobs Sr., who ran one of the largest businesses in Buffalo, wrote a letter to our chairman offering his support.[7]

As you build relationships with your champions, recognize the different types of roles they play. Some supporters are constantly by your side, helping you fight the everyday battles. Others may give you only a few hours (or even just minutes) each year, but they're there when the stakes are highest or when they can have the greatest impact.

Of course, even your most loyal allies can quickly turn into critics when your interests don't align. It's important to work with key stakeholders from the beginning to manage their expectations, prepare them for what's going to happen, and build relationships that can withstand the inevitable bumps in the road. I tell our board that most of our initiatives aren't expected to be profitable for years—if at all—so it's no surprise when they're not contributing to our bottom line in year one. Be honest with your allies. Let them know that things may not happen quickly or perfectly (let alone both).

Make a Decision and Move On

Not everything ends up with a handshake and smiles all around. There are times when you simply have to accept criticism, make a decision, and keep leading the way anyway.

Rev. Vincent M. Cooke was the president of Canisius College, a local, well-respected Jesuit institution. As head of the college, Father Cooke was involved in numerous successful real estate development ventures in town, including purchasing an old Sears Roebuck facility for the college to use, as well as multiple student housing facilities.

With a bachelor's degree, two master's degrees, two advanced theology degrees, and a doctorate degree, Father Cooke was probably the most well-educated advisor we met with. But perhaps his most important contribution was his plain-spoken advice for working with critics.

He told us that he thought our ideas for the medical campus were good but that Buffalo was a tough town for change. He said that given the scope of what we were trying to do, we'd inevitably run into obstacles, no matter how thorough, smart, and nice we were. Some of our ideas would simply be stonewalled. And when they were, we should just make a decision and move on.

His point was that we could stand there and ram our heads against the wall, or we could take action and then go work on one of the countless other good ideas that we needed to pursue. By moving on, we didn't waste our valuable time and energy fighting battles we couldn't win. (Of course, we were careful not to burn bridges, because often the same people who opposed us in the beginning wanted to partner with us when they saw our success.)

You can't wait to make a decision until everyone agrees with you, because if you do you'll never get anything done. Being a good leader doesn't mean dismissing resistance. It means acknowledging it and being willing to lead people in addressing it. Leadership means making decisions knowing that someone is probably going to be disappointed or angry no matter what you decide. You won't always be right. But leaders need to make difficult choices, and leadership is often the key difference when dealing with obstacles.

Be Your Own Critic

Sometimes you have to be your own critic by acknowledging and embracing failure.

At one point, we decided to take the lights in our main parking lot off the electric grid by adding solar panels and wind turbines to them. The project was a huge success—until just a few years later, when the lights stopped working, and we had to quickly hook them back up to the grid just so we could see our cars at night.

If you're involved in innovation, you're going to fail at times; that's part of the process. So when the parking lot lights stopped working, we didn't try to hide the problem. We contacted some local engineering students and asked for help. Ultimately, we couldn't fix the problem, but we left the solar panels and turbines up as a reminder that we tried, failed, and moved on. As an innovation district, it's important that we lead by example—whether that's embracing alternative energy or being honest about our failures. (And if you're really sensitive about your mistakes, just call them "prototypes," which we'll talk about more in chapter 8.)

Although it's easy to get worn down by critics, it's important to remember that when you're working to advance equity, you're fighting the good fight. If someone is trying to perpetuate income inequality or promote racism, it's your job—and your moral imperative—to argue, resist, and fight. Sometimes conflict is inevitable. Often, it's helpful. As Rep. John Lewis said, "Never, ever be afraid to make some noise and get in good trouble, necessary trouble."[8]

When you're facing off with opponents, I also urge you to engage in "principled conflict" by acting with integrity, addressing issues directly, and recognizing the value of ongoing relationships.[9] Fighting dirty may let you get in a few punches, but it's not a strategy for long-term success.

No matter how well you do your job, you're always going to have critics. When we started working on the medical campus, we probably had 90 percent of the people in surrounding communities not trusting us. Now, I'd say only 10 percent of them don't trust us. The dynamic nature of cities, anchor institutions, and innovation districts means that there will always be obstacles. People in marginalized communities, who we want to be most engaged, will often feel left out or left behind given that they have historically been overlooked. But in many cases, you can find common ground and work together for the good of the community. And, as we'll talk about in the next chapter, it all starts with listening.

CHAPTER 2
Ideas Must Be Good
for Most of the People

In the early days of the Buffalo Niagara Medical Campus (BNMC), some business leaders weren't convinced that the surrounding communities should be represented on the board of directors. The issue came to a head at a roundtable meeting, when one person voiced his opposition. "What do the neighborhoods have to do with this?" he asked. "We're building a medical campus. Whatever we're doing is going to be good for them."

As everyone sat quietly and let these words sink in, Angelo "Ange" Fatta stood up. Fatta, a respected businessman, accomplished singer, and one of our first volunteers, knew how to command an audience. "With all due respect," he said, "look around this table. None of us know what it's like to live in these neighborhoods." Without input from the people who lived right next door, Fatta argued, the campus could never reach its full potential.

Fatta's colleagues agreed, which is why we've had representatives from the adjacent neighborhoods (often the leaders of the respective community associations) on the board of directors since our inception.

Historically, anchor institutions and innovation districts have focused on their own needs first. It's somewhat understandable, given the size of these organizations and their unique nature. The problem is that many anchors and innovation districts make plans without fully considering what's best for everyone else. Hospitals, universities, and other organizations simply assume that what's good for them is good for the city. And in some cases, that's true. But good isn't always good enough, and good for the city doesn't mean good for everyone.

Many leaders at anchor institutions and innovation districts assume that what they're doing is good for everyone because they have good intentions, and the project is right for their organization. But you don't *really* know if it's best for everyone unless you have the community's involvement. That's where social design comes in.

The Principles of Social Design

Social design is a system based on inclusivity. Groups that follow the principles of social design ensure that their actions benefit most people, not just the select few; it's a philosophy captured in the title of this chapter ("Ideas Must Be Good for Most of the People"), a quote from social design expert Cheryl Heller.[1]

Social design "begins with why you want to change something, not what you want to change," writes Heller. "It makes the first order of business to identify the highest-level need."[2] When you follow the social design process, you're more interested in questions than answers. You flatten hierarchies and reconsider the definition of an expert. You listen to people's stories and learn to see your neighbors for who they really are and what they are capable of. You build powerful relationships, create consensus from the ground up, and implement ideas based on the actual (not simply perceived) needs of the community. The principles of social design give us a framework for discovering, understanding, and addressing the traditionally unmet wants and needs of underserved communities. Social design, notes Heller, "succeeds when all participants feel ownership of the process."[3] I won't go into all the details of the process here; instead, I'll focus on how anchor institutions and innovation districts can use social design to promote equity.

Who Are You Designing For?

At its core, social design requires that you consistently question who your plans will help—and, just as importantly, who your plans will hurt. For example, consider automobiles, which contribute to deadly air pollution, discourage density, and inhibit walkability. Yet for decades cities have prioritized cars and drivers, turning over acres of land for roads and parking while forcing pedestrians onto narrow sidewalks and crosswalks. If we were designing a city from scratch by following the social design process, it's doubtful we would come up with a model that is so harmful to so many.

As you're gathering input and making decisions, consider who you're prioritizing. In your model, who are the cars and trucks that you've traditionally designed for? Who are the pedestrians relegated to sidewalks?

Yes, these are complex issues, but that doesn't mean you're the only one who can understand, manage, and solve them. The people who live in the neighborhood around your anchor institution or innovation district know more about their neighborhood than you ever will. They are the experts.

Ignoring audiences isn't always intentional. But it does take an intentional effort to be inclusive. Consider how many women were involved with the design of your buildings and surrounding areas. Did people with disabilities help plan your local parks? How did you incorporate the needs of older people when developing programming? Your process is a reflection of your values. It's difficult to advance equity for all when you're considering only the perspective of a select few.

Introducing It to Leaders

When you introduce social design to key stakeholders in your organization, you're likely to face some opposition. Nobody wants something else added to their to-do list, especially if it's a process that takes more time and involves more people. But the bigger issue, in my experience, is that people are hesitant to embrace a process that isn't focused on their priorities.

Leaders will say that they don't want people outside the organization making decisions for them. That's understandable, but social design doesn't mean you give up autonomy. Although the community has input and influence, ultimately each organization decides how to proceed. Don't think of it as the community making decisions for the organization; think of it as the organization making decisions that also work for the community.

If you're an anchor institution or innovation district, you're going to have to work with the community. You can do it at the beginning, or you can do it after you've made your decision. Imagine you're having a party at your home. You can let all your neighbors know ahead of time and invite them to join you, or you can ignore them and hope they don't call the police when the music gets too loud. It's your choice.

Start with the Problem, Not the Solution

When you're trying to find ideas that are good for most of the people, it's easy to slip into the mode of gathering ideas and trying to figure out which one is best. But social design, as you'll recall, is about *why* you want to change, not *what* you want to change.

"We're used to solving problems," said Lucy Kerman, senior vice provost of university and community partnerships at Drexel University. "So we walk in and say, 'we have a solution.' They say, 'you have the wrong problem.'"

As is often the case, listening to other people can help you identify the right problem, even for institutions that have a long history of working successfully with the community. In theory, universities may be particularly well suited to problem solving; in practice, however, many of them lack the humility to recognize that, as Kerman says, "not only do they not have the answers—they don't know the questions."

Here in Buffalo, we're learning to take a problem-first approach. When we began advocating to bring the EforAll program (a nationally recognized model for equity in entrepreneurship) to Buffalo, we did so because we recognized the problems that cause small businesses to fail, including knowing how to create financial statements and how to file a business plan. These aren't sexy topics. People aren't beating down our door to sign up for seminars about legal structure. But we're not trying to attract a crowd or get headlines or impress people. We're trying to solve the right problem: how to get more small businesses to survive—and thrive.

Focus on Empathy

Empathy is a natural part of the social design process. In social design, you listen—really listen—to what other people are saying and recognize that they know their world better than you ever will. You connect with people whose experiences are different from yours. The word *empathy* has its origin in a root that means "to suffer."[4] When you're making decisions that will affect the community, ask yourself (and others), "Who will suffer as a result of our actions?" Our staff is taking courses in diversity and innovation, so all of us (including new hires) have a deeper understanding of each other. Although our goal is ultimately to advance equity (which requires empathy), it's important that we respect marginalized community members as equals rather than viewing them as people who need to be helped.

Consider Your Common Purpose

When I played basketball in high school, the goal was simple: win the game by getting more points than the opponents. Ultimately, it didn't really matter whether we made three-pointers or foul shots, as long as we ended up with more points than the other guys.

The social design process helps you find a common purpose with others. When you share a goal, you can put aside your differences and work together. But don't confuse the need for a common purpose with a desire for consensus, which can lead to compromise. Trying to get everyone to agree on a plan has the potential to water down your ideas. For example, a healthcare system and a community group may both want to improve people's health. That's a common purpose. But the healthcare system might say that the best way to improve health is to build a big new hospital, whereas the community group might propose a network of local clinics. If the organizations focus on building consensus through compromise, the healthcare system might agree to a smaller hospital, and the community group might agree to just a few clinics. But just because it's a compromise doesn't mean that's what's best for the community. Agree on a common purpose, and then evaluate plans against that shared goal.

Ask Why

Perhaps the most underrated exercise we use in social design is the five whys—literally asking "why?" five times to get to the root of the matter.

For example, when we developed our Healthy Corner Store initiative, we started by noting that people in low-income communities (including those near our campus) have higher rates of heart disease.

Why? In part because they aren't eating enough vegetables.

Why? They don't have places to buy fresh vegetables.

Why? The corner stores that serve those neighborhoods don't typically stock and sell many fresh vegetables.

Why? Fresh vegetables aren't typically as profitable for corner stores.

Why? Store owners don't always know the most effective ways to buy, package, and sell fresh vegetables.

Armed with this knowledge, our Healthy Corner Store initiative helped teach store owners how to find (and purchase) seasonal vegetables, how to rotate produce, how to package cut vegetables that are easy for people to buy, and even how to use leftover lettuce, onions, and other vegetables at their deli counter.

The beauty of this process is that it gets past the superficial issues and makes us really think about the root cause of the problem—and hopefully find a solution that we can apply broadly to affect change. It's the difference between saying, "People get heart disease because they don't eat healthy foods" (which assigns a scapegoat and makes the problem all but impossible to solve) and saying, "People get heart disease because corner store owners need training on how to prep vegetables to sell profitably" (which is a specific problem we can work together to address). (When you do uncover the problem, I find it's very helpful to write out—in plain language—what each group is looking for, which makes it easier to identify areas of potential conflict.)

As you ask these (and other) questions, be very careful about the language you use. What's nice about the five whys approach is that it helps you avoid asking leading questions that can influence the answer. For example, you're not asking, "Is the reason the corner stores don't stock fresh vegetables because those items don't sell as well as chips and soda?" You're just asking why the stores don't stock fresh vegetables, which lets you get to a more useful answer.

Gathering Input

Social design is about bringing people together and helping everyone understand what everyone else needs. As Heller wrote, it's not enough to see communities; "it's more important to understand how the communities see themselves."[5]

When I was starting to build relationships in one of the adjacent neighborhoods, I went to all their community meetings for about a year and just listened. I noticed that other people from outside the community would come in and give presentations about things like reverse mortgages. But the people from the neighborhood were trying to figure out how to get their trees trimmed and their potholes fixed. There's certainly a need to close the wealth gap, but part of social design is focusing on what people say is most important for themselves, not what you think is most important for them.

People want to be heard. People need to be heard. But listening to people isn't something that just happens. You need to actively create opportunities for community input and engagement. You can do this on a project basis, every time there's a new initiative. You can do it proactively, to have the community guide you on what you should be doing next. And you can do it as part of your structure, for example by engaging the community as part of your board of directors.

Of course, even before you reach out to others, you may find people reaching out to you. When a local pastor started hearing from his members about problems with the growing medical campus, he asked us to meet with a small group of his fellow clergy. They gave us an earful at that first meeting, talking about parking, jobs, and other issues that affected people's lives. That initial group of pastors transformed into the

Better Together leaders, a few dozen religious leaders representing different parts of the city. We'd meet once a month for lunch, and everyone would start talking about what they wanted. Usually by the time we finished lunch, we'd realize that we were all working toward a similar goal.

Traditional community forums, online surveys, and other ways of gathering input tend to attract people who actively want to share their voices and have the resources to do so. But they're not the only ones you should be listening to—even though it's more difficult to reach further out into the community. Ask yourself, "Who are the people who aren't engaged? Why aren't they engaged? And how can you engage them?"

Asking people questions doesn't mean they'll have the answers. But what they can give you is insight about their lives and their world—so that together you can make better decisions.

Eliminate Obstacles

If you want to talk with other people, you have to start by getting out into the community. That sounds obvious, but some people still think you can do everything from your office, hiding behind your laptop, when the people whose opinions you need the most aren't even in your building.

If you can, bring your ideas to the people rather than asking them to come to you. For inspiration, I look at programs like the University at Buffalo (UB) Mobile Dental Van, which brings dental care to rural areas of our community, or the UB HEALS street medicine outreach program, which sends medical students and faculty to help the homeless and others in downtown Buffalo. These types of programs, which exist in many communities, often provide proven models for outreach, even with hard-to-reach audiences.

Just because you're in the community doesn't mean you're speaking the right language. Find out how your audience prefers to communicate, then use those tools to spread your message. Don't assume that everyone communicates the same way you do. For example, officials in San Antonio found that approximately one in five households couldn't access online surveys, in part because they lacked internet access but also because of language barriers and problems with the language used to categorize respondents' ethnicity and other data.[6] In Philadelphia, Lucy Kerman noted that remote meetings due to COVID-19 placed an additional burden on people who "didn't have computers, high-speed internet, or simply enough minutes on their cell phones to participate in meetings."

As you think about who should be participating in the process, make sure you're looking ahead and thinking in aspirational terms. For example, when we're planning new spaces for entrepreneurs, we know that women aren't traditionally well represented in this area, which means we need to be intentional about ensuring that women have a larger voice in designing spaces that make them feel comfortable and welcomed.

When you're gathering input, you may have to experiment. There isn't a one-size-fits-all approach. As David Gamble (the architect who helped develop our master plan) noted, you need one-on-one conversations, large public meetings, and everything in between. You have to provide multiple feedback loops to make sure people are recognized, are engaged, and can influence the process.

I shouldn't have to even say this, but please don't hold performative engagement and listening sessions when the decisions have already been made. And make sure you're not just doing social design for the optics. People see through a charade. Do what's right for the community, not just what looks good in your annual report or on the news.

Social design is not a fast process. If you need to do something quickly, then social design isn't for you. It's not just about people speaking up at a public meeting and having their two minutes at the microphone. It's about them being part of the process from the beginning and having an open line of communication at every step. You don't just listen and then you're done. But remember: It's worth the time, and if you don't spend the time working with the community up front, you'll probably spend even more time battling them in the years to come.

Win–Win Isn't Always Achievable

Don't mistake "ideas must be good for most of the people" with "ideas must be good for *all* of the people." There will be conflicts. There will be disagreement. There will be people who aren't happy with the final outcome, even if it's still leading toward a common purpose.

The needs of the community are often in direct opposition to the needs of anchor institutions and innovation districts. In Buffalo, many of the healthcare facilities on our medical campus are directly adjacent to low-income neighborhoods. As these institutions expand and grow to serve the community, they often do so in a way that negatively affects the neighborhood, including higher rents and more traffic. We can't stop growth. But cities can have policies in place to help prevent displacement and other consequences, anchor institutions and innovation districts can support these policies, and leaders can think proactively about the effects of their actions.

Although our goal is usually to achieve win–win scenarios, we understand that urban development doesn't always work this way; "gentrification almost always takes place on top of someone else's loss," as one author put it.[7] But zero-sum thinking—in which one person's gain is based on someone else's loss—is one reason why we've ended up with inequitable societies. Even as we accept that not every idea can be each person's preferred outcome, we strive for fair and equitable solutions, in which nobody has to lose in order for everyone to win. For example, when we raised funds to improve the streets, sidewalks, and lights in the innovation district, we worked with supporters and the adjacent communities to make sure the money would also be used to make improvements throughout the surrounding neighborhoods.

Uncomfortable Truths

I can tell you firsthand that social design is a humbling process, especially for CEOs and others accustomed to getting their way. You give up power. You realize you don't know what you thought you knew. You discover that your best intentions weren't good enough. And you find that other people already have the answers to problems you've been working on for years.

Social design is a fundamental shift in how most organizations act, and therefore it can be disconcerting, especially at first. But embracing this approach is essential for communities and organizations that are working to address inequity. After all, if your ideas *aren't* good for most of the people, why are you moving forward with them?

When you don't think of others as your equals (or think of them at all), you can fool yourself into thinking everything is fine. Ignorance, as they say, is bliss. But once you fully open your eyes, the issues are clear. "If you acknowledge that their lives exist and that they matter, then it becomes immediately obvious something is terribly wrong."[8]

Social design doesn't eliminate obstacles. If anything, it brings them to the forefront and encourages participants to find ways, together, to overcome them.

The process inherently exposes the different motives of various groups and organizations. With social design, we don't shy away from the historical (and ongoing) tension between cities and anchor institutions, for example. Anchors, as per their name, tend to stay where they are. They can't just pick up and move, which is one reason why leaders of anchor institutions tend to make decisions that are focused on a longer timeframe. Communities are even more rooted in place. On the other hand, elected officials often focus on two- or four-year increments. Most mayors have little incentive to think twenty years into the future. Cities are also built on growth, regardless of whether this growth is in the best interests of the existing community (let alone whether it leads to greater equity).

In addition, by bringing opponents together, you create situations that may be uncomfortable for those who aren't accustomed to facing blunt criticism. Let's face it: You're not going to like everything you hear—about you, your organization, or your plans. If you're the type of person who shies away from conflict, then it may take you some time to get accustomed to social design. It's also important to understand that others may not trust you, especially right away, often because of historical issues and tensions between various groups (something we'll talk more about in chapter 6).

Here's my advice: Remember that most people are on your side. They want what you want, whether it's a better standard of living for people in the community, more walkable neighborhoods, or any other equity-related outcome. In most cases, you just disagree about how to balance these equity-related outcomes with business goals and about what each group is willing to give up in order to achieve a common purpose.

The results of not following the social design process are apparent in every city around the world. The demolition of the original Penn Station in New York City might be the classic example of what happens when decision makers don't consider the needs of the community, but a quick walk around your city will probably reveal numerous examples.

At the BNMC, we didn't always follow the social design system, and we didn't always listen to the community. In the beginning, we were just running programs, putting our heads down, and going full speed, without fully considering what people wanted or needed. And we—and the community—were worse off because of it. For example, even though each of the adjacent communities has had a seat on our board since the beginning, we assumed that just by having someone on our board from the surrounding neighborhoods, we would get all the input we needed from these neighborhoods.

Looking back, it's obvious how wrong we were. One representative—whether they're a shop owner, community activist, or anyone else—can't possibly speak for the whole community. Which is why, today, we partner in a variety of ways with the local neighborhoods to try and cast a broader net and make sure we're listening to as many people as possible.

What Is a "Good" Idea?

Finally, when we say ideas must be good for most of the people, what exactly does that mean? Even "good" ideas aren't likely to be equally good for 100 percent of the people. Where do you draw the line? Is it acceptable for an idea to be great for 70 percent of the people and just okay for 30 percent? What if the idea is sort of good for 90 percent of the people but horrible for 10 percent of the people? Does it make a difference if those 10 percent are in a wealthy suburb rather than a low-income neighborhood in the city?

Economic impact is a crucial measure but certainly not the only measure (let alone the best measure) of how good an idea is, especially if the economic impact will simply provide more riches to those who are already well-off. And even when there is a significant positive economic impact, consider whether it comes with other costs. For example, a new manufacturing plant that pays twice the prevailing wage—but requires a round-the-clock fleet of trucks rumbling through a residential neighborhood— may provide financial gains to some while creating air pollution and a hazardous environment for all.

Ideas that are rooted in your own self-interest can still be good for most of the people. For example, hospital CEOs understand that when people in the community have jobs, they're in a better position to pay their medical bills, which helps the hospital's bottom line. It's in a hospital's best interest to support programs that create jobs—not only because more jobs help the community but because they help the hospital directly. In Philadelphia, the University City District created Project Rehab, a free program to help property owners remodel and repair their homes. Individual homeowners benefit through increased home value, local contractors and suppliers get renovation jobs, and the district as a whole reaps the collective benefits of a safer, more attractive community. In fact, Project Rehab has strengthened the area around University City by unlocking "nearly $18 million in real estate value," according to the group's website. Don't discount an idea just because it's in your organization's best interests.

Here's an interesting way to think about how good an idea is: If you had a celebration for each decision you made, who would attend? If most of the people in the community would come to a party to celebrate your new parks plan, you've probably done a pretty good job. If only a handful of elected officials would show up—and they'd have to walk through crowds of protesters to do so—then it's probably not best for most of the people.

If an idea is going to hurt a sizable portion of the community—especially if it's going to harm those who are traditionally overlooked and underserved—then it's probably not a great idea. But at some point, it's impossible to quantify, so you have to really think about empathy, focusing on a common purpose, and all the other lessons we've discussed in this chapter.

CHAPTER 3
Check Your Ego at the Door

Shortly after we announced Thomas Beecher Jr. as our first chairman of our board, he was approached by Mark Mendell, the head of an international architectural firm that was headquartered nearby.

Mendell pointed out—very politely—that Beecher didn't know what he was doing. In fact, Mendell was so convinced that Beecher needed help that he offered to pay for a well-known urban planner to visit Buffalo and offer recommendations, no strings attached. Beecher had served as chairman of the board for one of the city's largest hospitals and was one of the most trusted people in Buffalo, but he knew that he wasn't an expert at urban planning. So he gratefully accepted Mendell's offer to bring in Alex Krieger, whose firm ended up creating the master plan for the Buffalo Niagara Medical Campus (BNMC).

Beecher could have said "no." He could have brought in his own experts. But one of the reasons we asked Beecher to chair our board is because he put the community first—not his ego. In this chapter, we'll talk about how to build a collaborative culture, even when people aren't as willing to put their egos aside and work together.

At the Top

Anchor institutions and innovation districts are powerful organizations. They control land, buildings, jobs, and much more throughout the community. Think about the anchor institutions in your community and the impact and influence they have on everything, from the local housing market and restaurant scene to tax policy and media coverage.

Anchor institutions, innovation districts, and governments are run by powerful leaders. University presidents, hospital CEOs, and mayors wield significant influence within their organizations and throughout the community—as do pastors, neighborhood association leaders, and others. Of course, it's not just those at the top, especially in high-profile institutions. These types of organizations are filled with brilliant researchers, inventors, and strategists, all of whom have power. Whether you work in the zoning department at City Hall, in food procurement for a university, in the legal department for a hospital, or in human resources for a startup company, you probably have much more influence on your city (and advancing equity within it) than the average person in your community. As Jane Jacobs writes, "people who get marked with the planners' hex signs are pushed about, expropriated, and uprooted much as if they were the subjects of a conquering power."[1]

Along with power and influence often comes ego. Sometimes the ego is there before the person takes the job, and sometimes the ego grows as the person fills the role. As I noted in chapter 2, it can be especially challenging for people to follow the social design process, because it inherently strips away some of their power. Few people—especially those accustomed to being at the top of an organizational chart—willingly give up power. Yet that's exactly what has to happen in order to advance equity. And it starts with getting egos in check.

Start with Small Egos

If you can, start by working with people who don't have big egos. George DeTitta was CEO of the world-renowned Hauptman-Woodward Medical Research Institute (HWI), yet he took the bus to work every day (a rarity in Buffalo, where you'll find plentiful parking and a twenty-minute commute). Bruce A. Holm, who co-developed a drug that has helped rescue nearly 500,000 premature infants, would encourage his biggest rival to take the lead on a research project if it meant a better outcome for future patients. Tony Masiello, who was Buffalo's mayor when we started the campus, told me, "Our job in city government was to get everyone together—and then get the hell out of the way." Masiello, a star basketball player who was drafted by the Indiana Pacers but chose a career in politics instead, knew when to put his ego aside. Norma Nowak is a world-renowned researcher whose work contributed directly to the Human Genome Project; you can often find her speaking to students (especially young women), encouraging them to pursue their interest in science.

Look for people who lead by example—like the mayor of Ithaca, New York, who turned his parking spot into a mini-park for the community. And don't assume that the most powerful people are at the top of the org chart. Janet Penska, an associate vice president at the University at Buffalo, regularly planned meetings for us with junior staffers at the state legislature because she knew that the elected officials were smart enough to listen to the voices on their team. (Penska, Holm, and Nowak were also instrumental in helping secure funding for the medical campus.)

So much of the work that matters—the work that really makes a difference—happens behind the scenes. That healthy eating signage you see in a corner store? That took a year of work with local farmers, shop owners, and marketing agencies to pull together. Like an iceberg, which has 90 percent of its mass underwater, most of what we do goes unseen and unrecognized. If you're looking to boost your own ego, advancing equity probably isn't the best way to do it. But at the end of the day, it's some of the most rewarding work I've ever done.

Be Right, Not Righteous

"Who are we really doing this for?" That's a question I ask myself a lot. There are a lot of things we could do that would make us feel like we're really doing great work, but they wouldn't do much to help make the community better. It's easy to sit around a boardroom table and make decisions that make you feel good. Sometimes, I can already picture the positive headlines in the newspaper. But then I think about whether we're doing what's righteous or what's right. Beware of serving your own ego.

You read in the Introduction about the proverb displayed in our boardroom: "If you want to go fast, go alone. If you want to go far, go together." Ego is about going alone. When I worked for *Saturday Night Live*, we had some of the most famous comedians in the world on our staff and movie stars as guest hosts. But the show wasn't about any one person—it was about all of us, coming together.[2]

When you say, "We know what's best for the community," that's ego. Sure, you can get things done quickly that way. But it's rarely going to provide the best results, let alone equitable impact for everyone who will be affected. I'll talk more in chapter 5 about the benefits of working together, especially when you're trying to secure funding or political approval.

Beecher, our chairman emeritus, recalls a trip to the Texas Medical Center, where someone asked the head of the organization, "What is your job?" He answered that when two CEOs are on the ceiling arguing, his job is to bring them down and get them to work out an agreement.

A good leader—whether they're head of an innovation district, an anchor institution, or a unit within an organization—brings people together. Which is why it's so important to put trusted, well-respected leaders in place, especially at the top of an organization.

Many of the best leaders I've worked with don't have anything to prove. Sometimes it's because that's just who they are—they're just naturally confident and secure in their abilities and vision. In other cases, they've been successful and made an impact in their profession and the community. They've already proven themselves.

Throughout our history, we've benefitted tremendously from the services and expertise of our volunteers, many of whom have been businesspeople who were retired or near the end of their careers. Volunteers, as I'll write about more in chapter 11, can be exceptionally effective. They're not usually volunteering for personal gain. However, they're also a self-selected group of people who typically have the wealth (both financial resources and available time) to spend unpaid hours working toward a cause, which can limit the diversity of the group.

If you're going to get anything done, you need top leadership involved. For an innovation district, that typically means having the CEO of each anchor institution on the board of directors. Within a hospital, university, or government, top leadership might be the heads of each building, school, or department. (In Buffalo, we actually have the CEO and the board chair for each major anchor serve on the innovation district board; we've found this helps give a broader perspective.)

The CEOs are rarely going to be the ones actually developing strategies and implementing equity-focused solutions, which is why you need to work closely with their support staff to get things done. Early on, we formed subcommittees and populated them with people from our member institutions who were specialists in things like safety, maintenance, public relations, and legislative affairs. In addition to taking advantage of their expertise, this allowed us to broaden our base of support. "When we brought in staff people with individuals below the C-level," recalled Bill Joyce, one of our former chairmen, "we started to get total organizational buy-in, and not just buy-in from the top."

Of course, one way to keep egos in check is to not hire people with huge egos in the first place. If you have the opportunity, take a close look at your recruiting and hiring process. If I were hiring someone for a senior leadership position at a hospital or other anchor institution, I'd have them meet with people throughout the community as part of the interview process and see how well they interact with the people they'll be serving, not just the people on your board of directors. And when you're looking for top leadership for an innovation district, consider the advice of Dennis Lower, the former CEO of Cortex innovation district, who said you want someone who is "attuned to lifting all boats—and not just the yachts."

One sign that you're working with the right people is that they care more about what they're doing than where they're sitting. Our first office space for the BNMC was literally in the basement of Roswell Park Comprehensive Cancer Center, one of our member organizations. The CEO let us work there, probably assuming we'd stay out of everyone's way. There was a small window way up high that let in some sunshine, but it was a far cry from the plush corner offices that many of our board members were accustomed to—which, in my mind, was perfect. It kept us humble, made us focus on the work, and helped weed out anyone who was just there for the perks.

All that said, don't be afraid to lead. From the beginning, we were unapologetic in saying that we were going to bring together institutions and neighborhoods for the good of the community and that we wanted partners to join us. Leaders should be humble but not at the expense of their ability to lead.

Think Small

Bigger isn't necessarily better. Within our innovation district, the HWI has approximately sixty-five employees, compared with the largest hospital group, which employs 12,000. But HWI's institutional namesake was Herb Hauptman, the first mathematician to win the Nobel Prize in chemistry. The models he helped discover let researchers visualize how proteins interact and have been used worldwide to study "most of the pharmaceuticals we take today."[3] HWI's building was the first new construction on the BNMC. And their staff started Beakers and Beer, a networking series that now draws thousands of people each year. (Even their origin story stands out; the institute was established in 1956 through a gift from Ms. Helen Woodward Rivas, whose father purchased the formula for what would soon be known nationwide as Jell-O.)

We've also seen the rise of micro-anchors—companies and organizations throughout the city that have a significant impact in a specific neighborhood. Here in Buffalo, Harmac, a medical device manufacturer located in a primarily residential neighborhood, has taken numerous steps to improve the immediate area. Their "Bailey Green" plan includes purchasing abandoned houses and converting the land to green space, providing space for a youth mentoring program, and partnering with community groups including Habitat for Humanity, which has built nearly ten homes in the area. A few miles away, green energy company Viridi Parente took over part of a vacant auto parts manufacturing plant and is helping to create a community where people can walk to work again. "If you rebuild manufacturing, you're setting the economy up for decades," says Viridi Parente president Dennis Elsenbeck. "We want to invest in green innovation and achieve renewable energy goals, while also building a new economy." The company's commitment extends far beyond jobs and energy; when CEO Jon Williams learned that a local resident couldn't get to his dialysis appointment because the end of his driveway was blocked by snow, Williams sent people out to clear driveways and sidewalks throughout the neighborhood. It's a small gesture that makes an enormous impact for the community.

Managing Egos

You're never going to eliminate egos, so think about how to manage them. I try to pay attention to what matters most to people and make sure they get the spotlight when it's important. For example, elected officials often tout the number of new jobs in their district—so if there's a big jobs announcement, make sure you thank your elected officials in the press release, in the press conference, and in any interviews you give. It doesn't cost you anything to give credit to others. People who care most about advancing equity often don't care who gets the credit for it.

Don't Overlook the People Who Are Already There

Beware of your ego as it relates to other communities. As one author pointed out, people often refer to underserved communities as a "blank slate" or use other terms that essentially ignore the people who have lived there for generations.[4] Just because you've started thinking about them doesn't mean that nobody else cared about them before you.

For years, Buffalo's historic Fruit Belt neighborhood—a predominantly Black community with some of the city's highest poverty rates— was overlooked, forgotten, and outright ignored by most people who didn't live there. But, as with any neighborhood, the people who call it home obviously care a great deal about their community. The average homeowner has lived there for more than fifty years according to Stephanie Simeon, executive director of Heart of the City Neighborhoods. "These people are the true urban pioneers," she adds. Today, the Fruit

Belt is on the rise. Resilient residents are taking ownership and building for the future, from neighborhood planning to housing development.

Given that the BNMC is adjacent to the Fruit Belt, I've been fortunate enough to meet with many residents, including women like Myrtle Davis and Altheria Ware, who spent countless hours going door to door, organizing neighborhood cleanups, talking with developers, and founding the Fruit Belt Friendly Block Club as a way to raise their collective voices.

The Fruit Belt—which takes its name from Grape Street, Orange Street, and other streets named for orchards planted in the mid-1800s—existed long before the campus did. I never want to forget that, so when we built our offices for the medical campus, we made sure that the main conference room on each floor included a panoramic view of the Fruit Belt neighborhood rather than the campus.

Don't Assume You Know Everything

Part of the problem with egos is that they trick us into thinking we know more than we really do. But social design, which I wrote about in chapter 2, requires that we do the exact opposite. "Social design requires a kind of ignorance," writes Cheryl Heller.[5] The smartest people I work with are the ones who know that they don't know everything. They ask questions—lots of questions.

When I asked our chairman emeritus, Tom Beecher, why he thought he was successful in the role, he said it's because "I don't go into something collaborative thinking I've got the answer, and that I have to convince people that this is what we have to do." Remember, it's okay to not have the answer right away. Uncertainty is part of the process. This may be disconcerting to straight-A students and overachievers, but if you insist on knowing everything all the time, you're going to be wrong more often than if you took the time to get to the real answers.

Admittedly, staying humble gets harder as you become more successful, both individually and institutionally. When we were just starting the BNMC, it was very easy to tell people we didn't know what we were doing, because, quite honestly, we didn't. Today, with a campus that's home to nearly 16,000 jobs, world-class research centers, and some of the best clinical care in the region, it would be easy to think that we have all the answers. We know more now than we did then, but we certainly don't know everything, as both our detractors and our supporters would be happy to tell you.

Surprise!

Part of checking your ego is keeping an open mind and not relying on conventional wisdom or assumptions. For example, did you know that new grocery stores don't always improve eating habits in food deserts?[6] Or that intersections that seem the most dangerous are actually some of the safest around?[7] Even things that seem comparable aren't necessarily so. For example, when it comes to economic development, one author found, "Streetcars stimulate investment and buses don't."[8] Of course, there are positive surprises, too. For example, green spaces can literally lower your heart rate.[9] And when Zipcar added cars in low-income areas, they often produced the most revenue.[10]

Many of these head-scratchers can be explained by digging into human behavior. Those "dangerous" nonstandard intersections, for example, actually cause people to slow down (because they're different) and pay more attention to what they're doing. Others require a comprehensive understanding of a process. But the point is that just because an idea may seem good (or bad) doesn't mean it truly is. You need to challenge assumptions. Dig deeper. Recognize that we're typically dealing with complex issues that are often intertwined. And ignore the voice in your head telling you that you already know the answer.

Adjust for Your Biases

Biases are especially harmful in terms of promoting equity, which is why it's important not only to recognize that you have them but to work intentionally to overcome them and find ways to eliminate the source of the bias. In Philadelphia, for example, a blind application process for an accelerator program helped reduce bias, resulting in multiple groups in which more than half of the companies were women- and minority-founded.[11]

If you assume you're not biased, you're wrong. If you think you're smart and aware enough not to let your biases influence you, you're also mistaken. Take your ego out of the equation. Throughout the years, I've tried to mitigate my biases by taking diversity training and by surrounding myself with a smart, diverse team. I meet with groups throughout the community—including neighborhood associations, activists, religious leaders, and others—and encourage them to point out my blind spots. These actions don't necessarily eliminate my biases, but they help prevent them from affecting our work to advance equity.

Learn from Your Peers

Within a well-balanced innovation district, you'll typically find academics, businesspeople, and for-profit and nonprofit organizations, surrounded by communities filled with concerned and engaged citizens, all within a city that is governed by elected officials.

Regardless of which groups you're in, consider what you can learn from others—both in terms of actual knowledge and in different ways to approach problems. When I asked David Gamble (who helped develop the 2003 BNMC Master Plan and the 2009 Master Plan update) for his thoughts, he observed an inherent tension between teaching and practice. On one hand, people in the academy benefit from a critical lens that challenges assumptions and pushes boundaries. They have the privilege of distance to be visionary, but bold plans often stumble if there isn't a feasible way to implement the vision. Practitioners, on the other hand, work in the trenches and understand constraints, but a sensitivity to on-the-ground conditions can thwart ambition, which is instrumental to get people excited—a necessary step in creating substantive change. (Gamble is both a lecturer at the Graduate School of Design at Harvard University and principal of Gamble Associates, a private urban revitalization firm.)

Every group has its strengths and weaknesses. Consider how your unique perspective shapes your approach to advancing equity. How would you approach your job differently if you were an academic instead of a practitioner, or a community activist instead of an elected official?

Don't Assume You Know What Others Need and Want

One of the primary purposes of the social design process is to discover what others want—not assume it for them. It's certainly tempting to skip this process. As Heller notes, "In the short term, it can seem more efficient to decide what people need rather than take the time to talk with them about it, particularly if they're not fluent in the same language of culture, country, or industry."[12] But assuming what others want is the opposite of a collaborative approach. Even among institutions, you need to be aware that your needs may be very different from those of other organizations, even when it comes to similar initiatives such as job training or procurement. As Marilyn Swartz-Lloyd, former CEO of MASCO (the Medical Academic and Scientific Community Organization) in Boston, pointed out, "Most of the institutions would appreciate training for applicants that strengthens their verbal, writing, and technology skills. The health system organizations are not so interested in off-site training for particular medical specialties. It's hard to devise general medical secretary courses for a hospital, when each hospital needs something that's totally different and would prefer to do in-house training."

You don't know what obstacles other people are facing. Something that is an obvious barrier to them may not even be on your radar—and vice versa. Although some entrepreneurs take it for granted that they can walk into their bank and get a loan, we've found that nearly 90 percent of the minority population doesn't have access to capital to start or grow a business. In fact, one of the reasons we brought the EforAll program to Buffalo is because of the obstacles that exist for many residents of our city.

If you spend a significant amount of time addressing equity, this is an obvious point. You already know that inequities in society are often caused by these types of obstacles, so you're attuned to their presence—even when they don't affect you. But even today, many people still assume that their personal experience applies to everyone, or they don't even consider the fact (until someone points it out) that someone else's experience may be vastly different from their own.

For example, I walk into my office every day, in a building that is open to the public for programs, co-working space, meetings, pop-up farmers' markets, and more. We've been here, in this building, since 2009. To me, our Innovation Center is for everyone in the city. Yet I've met people who live a block away who never felt that the building was open for them (in part because of the imposing architecture, which was not designed to invite people in—something to note if you're building or renovating). That's their experience and their perspective, and it's my job to help address it. (One way to judge whether you're truly putting your ego aside is to put yourself in someone else's position and ask whether you're being fair. Not everybody is going to agree with every decision you make. But if they feel it's unfair, then you have problems.)

Of course, even when you understand what people want and need, it's important to understand *why*. In Philadelphia, for example, the University of Pennsylvania found that some minority contractors weren't getting construction contracts. Why? In part because they didn't have access to the unionized trades.[13] If you don't get to the root cause, you're only going to solve the symptom, not the problem.

CHAPTER 4
Build a Table of Trust

On the Buffalo Niagara Medical Campus—as in most innovation districts—many of the institutions compete with each other on a daily basis. In the beginning, we were struggling with how to get these competitors to open up and work together.

"Finally, at one meeting I just said, 'you know, everybody here has got plans for the future.'" recalls Thomas Beecher Jr., our chairman at the time. "I said, 'I know you don't want to share your competitive secrets with anybody. But to the extent you're doing something where we might do it better together, how do we get that out on the table?'"

We weren't asking hospitals to show us their marketing strategy for attracting patients with cancer. All we needed was for them to share anything that was critical to the future success of the campus.

It was quiet for a few moments, until one of the CEOs said, "Okay, if you show me your plans, I'll show you my plans." Everyone agreed. And at the next meeting, everyone brought a copy of their growth plans to the table to share with their competitors. It was the first big step in building what I call the Table of Trust.

Advancing equity in a community requires a culture of collaboration, not competition. Leaders need to put their differences aside and work with each other. A CEO in North Carolina summed it up perfectly when talking about his main rival, explaining, "We made up our minds that when it came to business we'd try to kill each other, which we spent 30 years trying to do. But when it came to the good of Charlotte, anything we could do to build the city, we'd cooperate fully and completely."[1]

Getting Leaders on Board

Understand and expect that there will be mistrust, especially at the beginning. First of all, you have to build trust between institutions that often compete with each other for customers, funding, and other resources. When we started the Buffalo Niagara Medical Campus, few of the people at the table fully trusted each other. Buffalo—a town once known for the towering grain silos on the Buffalo River—had become a city where organizations created virtual silos, isolating themselves and fighting for resources, recognition, and power. Smaller institutions told how they had been mistreated by the larger institutions in the past. The big institutions were constantly battling to stay on top. Everyone was wary of everyone else. For some of the board members, it was a risk to be associated with the fledgling innovation district.

Top leaders of each organization must also be willing to collaborate. If you don't have the active support of the CEOs, it's going to be very difficult to get anything substantial done. They probably won't be the ones doing the work, but they have to be at the table and prepared to sacrifice money and power (especially in the short term) for initiatives that provide long-term, community-wide benefits.

So where did we start? By selecting a chairman, Tom Beecher, who was trusted by business and community leaders because of his past experience. Everyone trusted Tom, which is how he got everyone to trust each other. (The Thomas R. Beecher, Jr. Innovation Center on our campus is named in honor of Tom and his countless accomplishments.) Similarly, getting trust from one group can help you earn trust from others. For example, when we're seeking funding or political approval for a major project, we'll typically start by working with our local representatives in the New York State Legislature. Once they're comfortable with our plans, they can endorse them to our senators and representatives in Congress, who want to know that the state representatives are on board before they offer their approval. Having an endorsement from a U.S. senator or congressperson then helps immensely when reaching out to build partnerships with businesses and secure grants from national foundations.

One strategy to help organizations get past their differences is to point out that their competition isn't always who they think it is. As one former CEO recalls, a board member once took him out to breakfast and helped broaden his perspective. "He actually saw, very accurately, that our competition was not across the street. It was in Cleveland, Pittsburgh, and New York City, and we should end our petty differences in Buffalo and start thinking much more boldly about how we work together to be as good as these other places."[2]

Recognizing that we were all on the same team helped us act like it. Cities compete for talent, funding, companies, and more—and anchor institutions and innovation districts play a significant role in this competition. (Even though we compete with other cities, I still routinely share information with my peers in other cities, and vice versa, so we can learn from each other's mistakes and successes.)

Earning the Community's Trust

"I heard Leslie Lynn Smith, former CEO of Epicenter Memphis, talk about how we need to have a mindset of working with, not for," recalls Sam Fiorello, president and CEO of Cortex Innovation Community.

Collaboration isn't just about competitors working together. Anchor institutions and innovation districts must also partner with elected officials and community representatives to achieve common goals.

Earning the community's trust is even more difficult than getting business rivals to play in the same sandbox. The reality is that anchor institutions and innovation districts don't always make for the best neighbors. We'll probably never eliminate the tension between anchor institutions and the community, especially given that anchors typically expand by going further into adjoining neighborhoods. After all, few people want to sit on their front porch and have a view of a fifteen-story glass skyscraper or have to fight for parking spots. But we can help address and alleviate the mistrust.

So where does this mistrust come from? To start with, in most cases we find that the community typically hasn't even been invited to the table, even though their input is vital to a social design–driven process. In addition, representatives from anchor institutions and innovation districts often don't have the same life experiences as people from the community. I don't think I know any CEOs of an anchor institution or innovation district who live in an adjacent low-income neighborhood.

Unlike innovation districts, anchor institutions are often more attuned to their place in the neighborhood because these institutions have often existed for many decades and are usually located in residential communities, as Lucy Kerman, senior vice provost for university and community partnerships at Drexel University, pointed out when we talked with her. For example, universities are typically very concerned with "town–gown" relations, given the number of students, faculty, and staff who typically live on campus or within a short walk. But even some of the country's most prestigious institutions have a history of racist actions and attitudes toward minorities and others. In the 1950s, for example, the University of Chicago had "a fund they could use for 'area protection'" against Black people.[3]

Where else does the mistrust come from? Given that many anchor institutions are hospitals and research universities, it's important to mention that the Black community often mistrusts these organizations, given the history of medical experimentation on Black people and the ongoing inequitable health outcomes in Black patients.[4] When we saw some Black residents in Buffalo and nationwide skeptical about the COVID-19 vaccine, it wasn't just because the vaccine was developed in record time; it was partly because they didn't trust that their government and healthcare institutions wouldn't lie to them again.

And sometimes, the distrust is exacerbated for reasons beyond the control of these institutions. Here in Buffalo, some residents of the Fruit Belt neighborhood adjacent to the innovation district were surprised to find that their neighborhood was called "Medical Park" on some apps and websites. A determined reporter discovered that the mapping error stemmed from a database that probably referenced one map from a planning office (not ours).[5]

As you're working to address inequity, take the time to study and understand its origins. In Buffalo's historically Black Fruit Belt neighborhood, for example, the poverty rate is due at least in part to historic redlining, in which banks denied mortgages to area homeowners. Inequity doesn't just happen. It's caused by the actions of people in the community, year after year.

There's also a halo effect that can spread mistrust. If one institution within an innovation district loses (or fails to gain) the trust of people in the community, then people may be more wary of every organization within the innovation district. Even within an anchor institution or city government, if one department or unit is mistrusted, that reputation often spreads to the others.

Coming to the table together doesn't mean that people who have been mistreated for generations can simply get past it. It can take years—if not decades—to build and rebuild these relationships, and even then there may always be some level of skepticism. You must constantly show, with your words and your actions, that you have the community's best interests in mind. As Sam Fiorello, president and CEO of Cortex Innovation Community, says, "Trust takes time."

Everything Starts with Structure

An organization's governance and structure affect nearly everything they do, from who makes decisions (and who doesn't) to the impact they'll have on the community. You need to have the tough conversations as early as possible about your governance and structure and the processes that are followed, because it's what allows everything else to fall into place.

We've learned (often the hard way) that if you just build and focus on your structure at the top of the org chart, you won't get buy-in from people at the bottom. And if you just build at the bottom, it won't work because the money is controlled at the top.

This advice applies to individual institutions, but it's even more important for innovation districts and other organizations that bring multiple groups together. In our innovation district, the people on our board of directors include everyone from the CEO of a billion-dollar healthcare system to a representative from one of the poorest neighborhoods in the city. Making sure there's a place for everyone at the table—and that they feel welcome there—is one of our greatest ongoing challenges.

When you build a Table of Trust, you may not always like what you hear. The late Jan Peters ("Miss Jan," as she was affectionately known) and her friend, Ruth Bryant, both served on the innovation district board as representatives of the Fruit Belt neighborhood. The women were well known for their community involvement. Bryant, a notable political activist, was in the audience for Dr. Martin Luther King Jr.'s historic speech in Buffalo and served on nearly a dozen boards of directors; Peters received numerous service awards and had led a merger of two of the country's oldest "settlement houses" to form the Buffalo Federation of Neighborhood Centers. Both women were founding members of the Buffalo Chapter of the National Coalition of 100 Black Women.

Throughout their tenures on the board, they rarely missed an opportunity to speak up for the community. I remember vividly one time when the chairman of one of the largest anchor institutions was talking about the surrounding neighborhood.

When he was done, Peters simply said, "When it comes to the community, you have no idea what you're talking about." The room went silent. "I don't think anybody had spoken to him like that in 50 years," recalled one observer.

What I love about that story is that Peters felt comfortable enough at the table—and with the governance we had in place—that she could call out the head of one of the largest institutions in the city. She was an equal to someone who ran a multi-million-dollar organization.

Treating Everyone Equally

Within our innovation district, our goal from the beginning was for everyone to be equal. This doesn't mean that everyone has an equal say in terms of what happens within individual organizations. Each organization and community is responsible for its own decisions. But how can you promote equity if certain partners are treated inequitably? Everyone needs to have access to information and opportunities and the ability to voice their opinions.

In any community, you're going to have power dynamics. Some institutions—typically those that are larger and better funded—will come to the table with more power than smaller institutions. The goal is to set up a governance and structure in a way that ensures these organizations won't overpower the others.

You have to treat organizations as equally as possible, even—or perhaps especially—when some are typically more powerful than the others. Finding that balance isn't always easy. In our innovation district, the three largest institutions—Kaleida Health, Roswell Park Comprehensive Cancer Center, and the University at Buffalo—had (by far) the most real estate, employees, and influence. By some measures, they were nearly two hundred times bigger than the smaller organizations. So on our board of directors, each of the big three had two votes, and the other institutions had one vote each. Although this isn't equal, it gives the smaller players a significant voice. We also supported so-called KRUBS dinners (named for the initials of Kaleida, Roswell, and UB), where senior leaders from the largest institutions would talk about ways to collaborate.

Community groups often feel as if they have even less power. We wanted to change that dynamic, so, from the beginning, representatives from the adjacent communities each had a full voting seat on our board of directors.

What we discovered is that when you bring all these organizations together, everyone has to step up, put their best foot forward, and bring something to the table. They have to earn each other's trust. And it works; when Hauptman-Woodward Medical Research Institute (one of the smallest organizations) outgrew their building and needed a new facility, they had the support of the campus behind them. They were the smallest institution on the board in terms of tangible assets, but they deliver world-class research, and they had earned everyone's respect. Is it a perfect system? No. But we did (and continue to do) our best to ensure that everyone is treated fairly.

Paying Your Dues

As a well-traveled attorney, the late Al Mugel saw firsthand how a medical campus transformed cities like Cleveland and Houston. Long before I started working in Buffalo, he brought together key stakeholders, including representatives from local hospitals and elected officials. Mugel paid for countless working lunches, led the team on fact-finding trips, and tried to build consensus for a medical campus in Buffalo.

And he failed.

As Mugel later explained, there were two key problems: too many people overall and not enough people with skin in the game. People came together, enjoyed a lunch, and then went on their way without doing anything. They had nothing to lose.

So a few years later, when I was brought in to help revive the efforts to establish a medical campus, we paid close attention to Mugel's advice. We limited the number of people at the table (especially the elected officials), and we charged annual dues for member institutions. The dues weren't overly burdensome—they ranged from perhaps $10,000 for the smallest institutions to $100,000 for the largest—but they helped ensure that the member institutions were committed to the project. With this smaller group of dues-paying members, everyone involved had something to lose—and, more importantly, something to gain.

Of course, having a financial stake isn't just for the institutions; it can help cement community support, too. In Philadelphia, the University of Pennsylvania helped arrange for new outdoor lighting throughout neighborhoods, as long as participating homeowners paid half the cost.[6] Asking residents to invest money isn't always appropriate—for example, we've helped provide solar panels for free—but finding ways to get everyone invested, in some way, is a very useful strategy.

Think about how many people will be involved in the governance, because you can't typically have everyone. In our innovation district, we have more than 150 organizations—which means 150 different people in charge. We can't put them all on our board of directors.

That said, one thing to watch out for is if any one group has too much influence, which can compromise your overall mission. Having multiple funders strengthens the overall group and helps avoid situations like we're seeing in one city, where a company that is one of innovation district's largest funders wants the organization to focus more on business development.[7]

What Is Your Purpose?

Early in our existence, we took a trip to the Texas Medical Center, where we learned how an innovation district could enhance the work of the member institutions without being a threat to them. The people who run the institutions within an innovation district are focused on saving and improving peoples' lives; they don't have much time or energy left for urban planning, parking, transportation, and other issues. Ideally, an innovation district provides services that all partners benefit from but that none of them is best suited to perform. Logistically, this includes things like campus-wide parking and safety. But it can (and should) also include a focus on equity, which isn't typically a core function of a hospital, university, or startup company but can be a key role for the overarching innovation district.

A Word about Government

I could write a whole book about the need for a cohesive, strategic, forward-thinking government. For a community, that's where everything starts. Elected officials set the tone with their budgets, their leadership, and their priorities. Here in Buffalo, the Honorable Byron Brown took office as the city's first Black mayor in 2006 and is now serving his fifth term as I write this. Although the influence of elected officials may not matter quite as much in superstar cities such as New York City and San Francisco, it can make or break cities such as Buffalo, Indianapolis, Phoenix, and dozens of others. Outside the United States, we've seen many cases in which significant government involvement has helped turn around struggling cities—including Medellín, Colombia. But here in the United States, for a variety of reasons, governments often take a secondary role in creating more equitable cities.

Be Intentional about Your Table

Once you have the right governance and structure, the most important thing is to get the right people at the table—people who are going to work together for the good of the community. Sometimes you can't choose these people; for example, it's important to have the CEOs on the board of an innovation district, regardless of their commitment to the community. But when you have a choice, think carefully.

Before you build your table, look for the people who are already doing the work. "Too many times people say let's create the table and invite them to our table," says Samina Raja, founder of the University at Buffalo Food Systems Planning and Community Lab and past advisor to the World Health Organization and the United Nations Food and Agriculture Organization. Instead, Raja suggests, "Maybe find out what tables already exist and find out how you can get invited to those existing tables, so you're starting from the ground up."[8]

Part of building a collaborative culture is making sure that your organization is balanced. For example, if there's too much of a corporate culture in your innovation district, that may make academics and startups feel like they're not as welcome. Balance extends to diversity, too. Are your partners diverse? Think beyond race and gender and consider age, sexual orientation, disabilities, and other factors. The more diverse they are, the more likely you'll be to collaborate on projects that address equity for the broadest range of residents. Of course, although diversity is important in terms of representation, make sure you're working with people who are truly community-minded and that you're not just building a diverse team for the optics.

Community Leaders

Unlike a business or nonprofit organization, there is no CEO of a neighborhood. Even the head of the block club probably doesn't represent everyone in the community, let alone have the authority to speak for them. Perhaps the best advice was what I heard from David Gamble, who told us to not just look for people who have demonstrated community leadership but also to think about what motives they might have to oppose others' ambitions. Try to pick future leaders who aren't currently at the table; for example, we're working with the Buffalo Urban League Young Professionals to bring some new voices into the mix.

Understand that it may be a risk for some people to partner with you. We've struggled at times to find leaders from different communities, especially minority communities, where residents might question why someone would want to partner with traditionally White-led organizations that, to be frank, haven't always had the best relationship with the surrounding neighborhoods. There's no quick fix for this. It takes time to build trust. Simply acknowledging that you know someone is taking a risk can also go a long way toward a strong partnership.

Understanding the motivations of the people at the table is extremely important when you are trying to build trust. Think about where their paycheck and status are coming from, because that will probably have a significant influence over their decision making, consciously or not. I've talked with so many people who have great ideas and say they'll lead a project, but at the end of the day they go back to where their paycheck comes from. But we wake up every morning, as an innovation district, and think about how we can advance equity in the community. Find people whose motivations are aligned with yours.

When I think back on our early success, one key factor—which happened largely by circumstance—was holding our board meetings in a neutral location. It would have been easy to meet in someone's executive conference room. Instead, we decided to hold our meetings in the reception area of a newly opened hotel. It was in a central location, the space was always available, and someone knew the manager. But the best part, in retrospect, is that it was neutral ground. Everyone, including community members, had to leave their offices to get there. It was a small but clear sign that we were all in this together.

Also, consider how the space you're using is set up. Are opponents literally on opposite sides of the table, or are they sitting next to each other? Are there rows of seats all facing the front of a room, or are chairs arranged so that everyone can see each other? Think about how your space makes people feel. (This advice applies to physical meetings, but there are certainly parallels to virtual collaborations. Be aware of the power dynamics, and try to arrange things so everyone is on equal footing.)

As you're building partnerships and inviting people to the table, remember that access alone does not ensure equity. We know this from education, healthcare, and other areas; for example, in one study, Black men were less likely to get a referral for specialized care than White men, even when they had the same doctors and insurance.[9] Just because people are at the same table doesn't mean they have the same voice.

Shared Goals and Values

Committing to a shared set of goals and values is a key step in building trust.

For example, in Los Angeles, the Transportation Electrification Partnership is working toward a 25 percent reduction in greenhouse gas emissions and air pollution by 2028, when Los Angeles hosts the Olympic and Paralympic Games. The partnership's members represent a wide range of interests, all united by this one goal; collaborators include representatives from industry (BMW Group and Tesla), utilities (Pacific

Gas & Electric), government (the Los Angeles Department of Water and Power), and academia (the USC Schwarzenegger Institute for State and Global Policy).[10]

But having a common goal isn't enough if you don't also share the same values. You're going to be most effective when everyone truly believes in collaboration. As in any strong relationship, partners should be open and honest, willing to share their information and resources.

Although it's never too late, it's certainly easier to follow through on your goals and values if they've been clear and decisive from the beginning. Innovation districts have an advantage here, given that most of these organizations are young or are still being established, and they don't have the history that many anchor institutions have. That said, even a two-hundred-year-old anchor institution can reinvent itself. Even if you have to change directions, it's better to start rebuilding trust tomorrow rather than keep going down the wrong path.

Be Open

Let's face it: Things are going to be awkward at first when you're asking competitors and people who don't trust each other to work together toward a common goal. For starters, simply talking about the issues can help. Have a conversation about the issues in your community, such as racism, gender inequities, displacement, food security, homelessness, or any other concerns. You may not be able to jump right into a heavy topic the first time you're all getting together, but ignoring the issues doesn't help anyone.

Share your failures and shortcomings to build trust. I often start conversations by telling people that Buffalo has the second-highest poverty rate for children among major U.S. cities and that we're one of the top twenty-five most segregated cities in the country.[11] When I meet with people who tell me about Buffalo's failures in advancing equity, I agree with them. Like most cities, we've had our opportunities. In the 1960s, the University at Buffalo decided to build a new campus in one of the city's suburbs rather than adding on to their existing city campus. This was a once-in-a-generation opportunity to improve equity on a significant scale (although there certainly would have been challenges, including avoiding displacement and gentrification). Fortunately, in recent years the university has renewed its commitment to the city by investing in a new medical school and other health-related facilities in the downtown innovation district, as well as creating programs specifically designed to advance equity. But we haven't done enough. Clearly we haven't solved all of the problems our community faces. We can always do more—as a community and as an innovation district.

It's also important to recognize that, as much as the community benefits from being at the table, their presence and input and insight help anchor institutions and innovation districts just as much—if not more. I've learned a tremendous amount about our community from the religious leaders and neighborhood representatives I've had the pleasure of working with, because we've spent decades building our relationships and establishing our mutual trust. They're the ones who help me avoid the landmines and navigate sensitive issues. If I need to make a decision now, they're some of the first people I call, to understand how our decision is going to affect the community.

Keeping People at the Table

At one of our early holiday parties, our chairman's wife asked one of the anchor institution CEOs if her husband (the chairman) was doing a good job. The CEO said that anybody can get people to the table, but her husband kept them there until they got something done. To this day, our chairman (now emeritus) says it's one of the best compliments he's ever received.

Keeping people, especially top leaders, at the table gets tougher as time goes on. Here in Buffalo and in other cities, I've seen people and organizations revert to their silos after they've achieved their initial goals. A facility gets built, some infrastructure is established, and people think their job is done. Governments also tend to retreat with time, often because they think things are on track and that someone else (either the anchor institution or the innovation district) is taking care of the day-to-day execution.

But you're not finished. Once you've done the work of building the table, don't let people back out—especially if you're focused on advancing equity. There's always more to accomplish. And it's probably going to get done faster—and better—if everyone stays engaged.

Finally, think about your next steps. Bringing partners together is great. But ultimately we want people to be able to connect themselves through integrated networks. Traditionally, organizations such as governments, anchor institutions, and corporations have held the power. People on the outside don't typically have easy access to the people and resources inside, unless they're invited in. An integrated network, on the other hand, brings together people from all sectors of society and, importantly, creates new connections between diverse groups. Integrated networks help eliminate gatekeepers and provide a much more efficient way for people throughout the community to work together. I'll talk more about integrated networks in chapter 10, but I wanted to mention them here, because they're what we hope to create as we build a collaborative culture.

CHAPTER 5
Speak with One Voice

"If you want our money, you'll have to work together."

That's essentially what The John R. Oishei Foundation told three separate anchor institutions when they asked for money to fund new buildings on the Buffalo Niagara Medical Campus (BNMC).

As Buffalo's largest foundation, Oishei has quietly supported the BNMC from the beginning. But all along, there was one steady condition: The institutions had to collaborate. Funding requests from individual organizations would almost invariably be rejected. Any request had to come from the campus as a whole.

Insisting that the institutions collaborate wasn't a popular decision. But it was the right one. And the leadership at Oishei knew they could leverage their financial power to make the most of the community's finite resources. "It made a lot of sense to take these significant assets and bring them together, because two and two makes five, every time," said Erland "Erkie" Kailbourne, chairman of the Oishei Foundation, backed by executive director Tom Baker. By focusing on the good of the entire community, Kailbourne and Baker lived up to the foundation's namesake, John R. Oishei, who was known for his loyalty to Buffalo. (Oishei invented the first automobile wiper blades and refused to move his company to Detroit despite pressure from Henry Ford himself.)

And it wasn't just the Oishei Foundation telling us we had to speak with one voice. Bob Kresse, Janet Day, and Tom Lunt at the Margaret L. Wendt Foundation—another early supporter—said the same thing. Even our state legislators basically refused to consider funding requests for one of the anchor institutions unless everyone in the innovation district was on board with the plans.

"People would say to us: 'Come back to us with a single plan, a single vision, a single ask,'" noted former Buffalo mayor Tony Masiello. "We heard that time in and time out from our Western New York delegation in Albany and certainly from our delegation in Washington."

Innovation districts and anchor institutions (including foundations) have the opportunity to help shape multiple voices into one cohesive vision, in large part because these organizations are often trusted and well established, with deep roots in the community. They have the resources to span neighborhoods, demographics, and other divides to bring people together, identify the common problems, and find solutions that advance equity. In this chapter, we'll talk about how they do it.

A Proven Approach

When I was helping develop a plan for the BNMC, my boss, Rick Reinhard, always said our job was to "keep everyone singing out of the same hymnal." So perhaps it's fitting that one of our first successes was an alliance with Pastor Michael Chapman.

Pastor Chapman was the leader of St. John Baptist Church, Buffalo's largest Black congregation. I remember going to meetings in the hallway outside his office, where he set up a table that probably sat fifteen or twenty and was often filled to capacity with people from throughout the city, eager to discuss Chapman's latest plans.

We partnered with Pastor Chapman for a grant from the Robert Wood Johnson Foundation and applied for the grant together. But we knew that there were probably 1,000 applicants vying for a few dozen or so awards. So when the foundation invited us to Baltimore to discuss our application, we happily got on a plane and went (although Pastor Chapman wasn't *quite* as excited about it, since he didn't like to fly). We walked into the room together, shared our vision, and thanked them for their time.

When we were chosen as one of the grant recipients, I asked the foundation what made us stand out. They said it was the fact that Pastor Chapman and the BNMC were true partners every step of the way. He wasn't just a name on the grant application. Honestly, I don't think they really believed that a medical campus could have an authentic collaboration with the community, especially one of the city's lowest-income neighborhoods. But in my mind it was the only way to succeed. Being on the same page was imperative if we wanted to change lives. So we went to the foundation—together—with one request and one common goal. And that made it easy for them to say yes.

A Broad Coalition

In Baton Rouge, a thirty-nine-year-old artist with schizophrenia died in jail, reportedly killed by a blood clot induced by the restraints placed on him by jailers.[1] The man's father, frustrated by a lack of coordinated mental health services throughout the community, started advocating for change.

For the next five years, a variety of partners including local physicians, the police chief, coroner, mental health advocates, and the district attorney all banded together for the cause. These people had diverse professions but shared one goal: secure funding for a facility designed to help people experiencing mental illness and related substance abuse issues.

After a number of setbacks, the funding proposal went to a ballot initiative and passed in a landslide, with nearly seven out of ten voters approving to fund the Bridge Center for Hope. "I'm just amazed. I never expected that type of support," said Kathy Kliebert, chairwoman of the Bridge Center, which can help up to five thousand people each year.[2]

Groups that don't typically work together can often find shared interests when it comes to advancing equity. If you're trying to garner support for a project, start by casting a broad net. Think about who may agree with your end goal, even if they aren't one of your typical partners.

Understand Why You Aren't on the Same Page

If people aren't speaking with one voice already, think about why not. Are they just accustomed to working in silos? Do they not know about each other's goals? Or are there more substantial differences you need to overcome? Your strategy and approach should depend on the answer.

When we launched our Farm-to-Hospital program to get more local produce into area hospitals, we helped bring together people whose motivations were different and who didn't always collaborate but who would all benefit from the project—much like the coalition from Baton Rouge. Healthcare professionals wanted patients to eat more nutritious food. Local farmers wanted to sell more of their crops. Hospital administrators and purchasing staff wanted to serve fresher food and lower their costs. They weren't opposed to working together; they just didn't know that they could. So, as an innovation district, we showed the farmers, healthcare professionals, and administrators that ultimately they all wanted the same thing—more local produce and dairy in hospitals—then got them to agree on a marketing campaign to promote the Farm-to-Hospital initiative.

In some cases, however, there's real opposition to speaking with one voice. Organizations may be wary of partnering with others, especially if they have a culture of noncollaboration or you're asking them to share a stage (and the spotlight) with their competitors. As you'll recall from the beginning of this chapter, when we tried to get local institutions to combine their funding requests into one ask, we faced a fair amount of pushback. It took the threat of losing funding for them to agree, at least at first.

You may also find that different groups have different problems they're trying to solve, which makes them resistant to collaboration. In the case of Boston's Muddy River daylighting project, the Army Corps of Engineers was tasked with improving flooding in a cost-efficient manner, while parks advocates wanted to see the river banks replanted to match Frederick Law Olmsted's vision—a much more time-intensive and costly proposition. The groups ended up finding a creative solution, but it wasn't easy given their conflicting goals. In these types of cases, start by making sure everyone understands each other's motivations. "Half the problem really is communication," said Tom Yardley, vice president at MASCO (the Medical Academic and Scientific Community Organization). "People's knee-jerk reaction is 'why aren't engineers addressing all these other needs?' The answer is more complex, because a scope of work for flood control is narrowly defined and wouldn't automatically include other needs such as road improvements."

There's no one-size-fits-all solution to getting everyone on the same page. It helps to be open and transparent about your goals and be clear about what you're willing to compromise on. The best advice I can offer is to be patient, ask questions (remember the "five whys"), and listen. Empathy goes a long way. Once you understand the real reasons *why* someone doesn't want to work together and how strongly they feel about their position, it's much easier to find a potential path to collaboration—or agree that there's not an opportunity to partner at this time.

And when you do agree on a message, make sure you're actually representing everyone. It's neither productive nor fair to speak with one voice if you're just repeating the loudest voice at your table or the voice that belongs to the most influential person. Make sure the message you're sharing is one that everyone can agree with.

What Brings People Together

Innovation districts (and other umbrella groups) play a unique role because they bring other institutions together and can elevate their individual voices. For member organizations, this is one of the main benefits of belonging to an innovation district. "We could speak with one voice with a heck of a lot more clout than if just one of us stated a problem," said Chris Greene, the former CEO of Hauptman-Woodward Medical Research Institute here in Buffalo.

Unfortunately, it often takes a precipitating crisis or major issue in the community to bring people together—and keep them together. After all, if there's no reason to come together, people tend to stay in their own silos and keep looking after their own best interests. In Buffalo, it took a prominent foundation threatening to withhold funding. In Medellín, Colombia, it took decades of drug wars.

By the end of the 1990s, drug-related violence dominated headlines in Medellín as Pablo Escobar and his cartel made billions of dollars trafficking cocaine. City leaders knew they had to transform their economy to save their community—and save lives. "Instead of rebuilding homes after a natural disaster, we were rebuilding society after a social disaster," noted Jorge Pérez Jaramillo, former chief planner of the city.[3]

Fortunately, people came together—the universities, private sector, and public sector—with a vision for an innovation-based economy that addressed inequity throughout the city. But it wasn't really a choice.

"If we don't offer good opportunities to young people here, then they go back to drug dealing," said Paulina Villa, manager of the city's Ruta N innovation district and a widely recognized leader in creating more equitable communities. It's a good lesson: Take advantage of the tipping points that force people to work toward a common goal.

Four Neighborhoods, One Community

To the east of the BNMC is the Fruit Belt neighborhood. To the west is Allentown. To the south is downtown. Although these communities are very different in terms of demographics and other factors, they all share a strong connection to the campus.

As the innovation district quickly grew, we realized we needed to have a common vision between the campus and the community. So when we updated our master plan, we hired a planning group to work directly with the neighborhoods. We talked to block club leaders, hosted community forums, and encouraged an integrated planning effort. The result was *Four Neighborhoods, One Community*, a 124-page document that continues to be an effective framework for collaborative engagement and empowering residents "to speak with one voice about the changes they would like to see in their neighborhoods."[4]

Four Neighborhoods, One Community wasn't a one-time effort to gain consensus. We're still constantly talking with the communities and hosting meetings. There are certainly disagreements between (and within) the neighborhoods about what's best for everyone, but keeping the communication channels open is crucial.

Give a Little to Get More

When it comes to getting everyone on the same page, you need leadership. Some of the most frustrating problems occur when a new leader comes into a city and doesn't have a collaborative mindset. Unfortunately, some leaders come in and have something to prove. That's when you get institutions vying against each other for resources and attention rather than joining together for the common good.

Yes, there are certainly instances when institutions have to make decisions on their own and go alone down a path. But in these cases, their long-term success usually depends on *how* they do it—whether they're still keeping the community at the forefront or whether they're focused only on their own bottom line or other internal measures.

(This is one reason why finding effective leadership is so important for anchor institutions and innovation districts. If you're going to invest time and resources somewhere, I'd recommend taking a close look at your hiring process and thinking about how you can use testing, community interviews, and other methods to identify potential leaders who already have a collaborative mindset.)

Another common breakdown point, related to leadership, is after you've had some success as a group. That's when people start to think they can achieve the same results on their own and begin to splinter off. It's funny, because when we first started the BNMC it was fairly easy to bring everyone together because, frankly, nobody thought much would come of it. So everyone was willing to come together and give it a shot. It's easy to think you know how to solve problems once you get a couple of wins. But you have to keep everyone at the table (as we discussed in chapter 4) and keep them speaking with one voice in order to get *continuous* wins. I've seen those struggles, when people thought they could go off on their own and achieve the same results that they accomplished together. Fortunately, once they realize that it's just not possible, they start to come back and appreciate the benefits of collaboration.

Everybody says they want to work together. But saying it is very different from doing it. You can't force people to agree on the same goals, of course. You may end up spending weeks, months, or years waiting on organizations that just aren't ready or willing to work together. That's okay. It's worth the wait. And in the meantime, there are usually plenty of people out there who are ready to collaborate.

A Word about Elected Officials

Speaking with one voice is crucial when you need something from your elected officials. When each organization is asking for its own funding or legislation, the elected officials can easily divide and conquer them. But when everyone is asking for the same thing, it's a lot harder for elected officials to say no.

Keep in mind that elected officials may also have to be on the same page with each other in order to be heard. Here in upstate New York, our state senators and assemblymembers are far outnumbered by elected officials from New York City. So the upstate contingent of Democrats and Republicans has to be united, determined, and laser-focused in their purpose. They need to put party affiliation aside and act as one voting bloc, which they did when convincing their colleagues to support the initial creation of the BNMC, with New York State as the largest single funder. Working together works.

Effective Communications

I was an English major at Hobart and William Smith Colleges, so the art of communication has always been near and dear to my heart. If you're going to speak with one voice, you need strong communication skills.

At a bare minimum, I encourage you to follow some best practices. Designate a spokesperson who's comfortable speaking to others. Develop shared talking points. Hire someone who specializes in the type of communication that you need. Many projects have failed because of a lack of effective communications.

There are specific communication challenges when it comes to equity, planning, and related fields. For example, consider that various groups often speak in different vocabularies. In a presentation about the Muddy River project in Boston, the U.S. Army Corps of Engineers writes like a bunch of fact-focused engineers; "Trees to be Planted Will Be representing 10 species. These include 77 oak, 40 maple, and 21 Tupelo."[5] A citizen-led beautification group, on the other hand, waxed poetic about the landscape, calling the river Olmsted's "pleasure route of parkways."[6]

Be wary of words and phrases that the general public doesn't understand. As the planner who coined the phrase "tactical urbanism" explains in his book by the same name, "We are the first to recognize that it's another example of planning jargon, and that puts distance between people and those who serve them."[7] In some fields and organizations, including universities, language is often used as a way of gatekeeping, which causes problems when you try to welcome people who aren't versed in the vernacular.

Think about how you're talking—especially about people—and how your words will be interpreted. For example, we try not to refer to disabled people but rather people with disabilities. The disability does not define the person, just as race does not define a person of color. It may seem like semantics, but it's a crucial distinction because it puts the focus on the person, not the situation.

Take a minute and reflect on the importance of effective communication. You can't start a relationship without it. You can't achieve equity without it. It's so important to recognize and respect our differences and do everything possible to make sure your choice of words isn't biased and that what you say won't be misinterpreted.

Write things down. Draw pictures, even if they're just whiteboard sketches of stick people. Make a diagram that tells your story. Especially once you're starting to crystallize a strategy or formulate a plan, putting something concrete in front of people is a great way to get feedback and gain consensus. You'll immediately start to see where there are disconnects and disagreements.

Don't be afraid to repeat yourself. Especially in the beginning, we probably gave hundreds of speeches talking to people throughout the community about what the medical campus would be and how it would affect their lives. Just because you've heard yourself explain something one hundred times doesn't mean other people have. I can almost guarantee that most people in your city probably don't know what your anchor institution or innovation district is doing to promote equity in your city. Keep sharing your message.

Approach new and emerging communication tools with caution. Social media lets you engage with audiences, but not everyone has access to a reliable internet connection. The newest platforms are often dominated by early adopters, who probably aren't a representative cross-section of people in your community (it doesn't matter if you're speaking with one voice if some people can't hear you). And with social media come concerns about privacy and increasing divisiveness. It's easy to rely on social media because it's essentially free and provides instant feedback, but I urge you to beware of the pitfalls.

Consider your existing regional narrative and how you and your organization fit into it. Here in Buffalo, we're proud of our blue-collar work ethic, our perseverance in dealing with adversity, and our ongoing role as the underdog. Although we've celebrated successes—from our startup ecosystem to downtown development—we recognize we still have a long way to go in terms of racial equity and other areas. You're probably not going to change your city's regional narrative by yourself—at least not overnight—so consider how you're aligning your communications with your city's story to establish a cohesive voice.

Finally, think about names. Often the first thing a group has to decide is what to call themselves, or what to name the project they're working on. Don't just pick the first one that sounds good. Your name is the first thing people hear about you. It's the first clue to help people understand who you are, what you do, and why they should care.

When we first started back in 2002, "innovation districts" weren't really a thing yet. So, after a considerable amount of debate, we decided to name ourselves the BNMC. (Buffalo is only a twenty-minute drive from world-famous Niagara Falls.) The name continues to serve us well, but it's interesting to see the new crop of innovation districts these days with names like 39 North in St. Louis and The Switch in Birmingham. I encourage you to think far ahead as you're brainstorming and choose a name that everyone will rally behind for years to come.

CHAPTER 6
Talk about Us (Not "Them")

One of our former chairmen, Bill Joyce, had a favorite saying: "You is us and they are we."

He explained that people would typically refer to a neighborhood, university, hospital, or other entity as "we" or "they," depending on whether they considered themselves part of the organization or not.

"It was really important," said Joyce, "to just say over and over again that it's not we or they—it's us. You is us, and they are we."

If anchor institutions, innovation districts, and the surrounding communities want to advance equity, we can't think in terms of "us" versus "them." Especially now, as parts of society become even more divided, anchor institutions and innovation districts have the power to bring people together and establish a culture that prioritizes community needs.

When I played basketball in high school, I was a point guard. I'd rather make a pass or get an assist than score a basket. For me, it's not about getting the credit. It's about getting the win. If your goal is to advance equity, you can't be focused on your individual accomplishments.

Unfortunately, what I've seen is that many anchor institutions and innovation districts choose not to address (let alone prioritize) the needs of the community, including the surrounding neighborhoods. Organizations are often too focused on their own plans, leading to what former Buffalo mayor Tony Masiello called, "a vision in a vacuum."

Anchor institutions and innovation districts can play a critical role in helping organizations see the big picture—not just in terms of logistical issues such as parking and safety but in terms of community-wide, equity-related needs.

Working with Others

Regardless of what type of organization you work for, you probably have to work with people and communities outside your group, even when you don't want to. This can cause tension when there are clear differences between the groups, for example, when there's an innovation district filled with high-earning employees adjacent to some of the city's lowest-income neighborhoods. If I'm being honest, I'll admit that there were times when we were tempted to stop working with certain people or groups simply because we weren't on the same page. We didn't agree with their position, and they probably felt the same about us. But walking away isn't an acceptable (or productive) solution. There were times we couldn't work with them right away, but we never dismissed the idea of ever working with them. Ultimately, it comes down to what you do have in common: your community.

If you're going to prioritize the community needs, one of the first things you need to do is understand exactly what you're talking about when you say "the community." To start with, what are the geographic borders? Are you just focusing on the immediate neighborhoods or taking a city-wide or even regional approach? In other words, when you say "us," who does that include?

As head of the innovation district, for example, I would say that "us" includes all our member institutions, everyone who works or studies within the district (regardless of where they live), and anyone who lives in Buffalo and the surrounding suburbs. That said, I recognize that we can have a much bigger impact on our closest neighbors (whether that's a positive influence such as improved public transit and parks or a negative one such as displacement), so that's where a lot of my attention goes.[1]

But don't just think in terms of geography. For example, when it snows here in Buffalo, we typically clear the highways and streets first, then the sidewalks. That's what most cities do. However, other cities consider gender equity when determining what to plow first, writes Leslie Kern in *Feminist City*. As a result, these cities prioritize "sidewalks, bike paths, bus lanes, and day care zones in recognition of the fact that women, children, and seniors are more likely to walk, bike, or use mass transit."[2]

The "us versus them" mindset doesn't just apply to one institution or neighborhood versus another. It's pedestrians versus drivers. Men versus women. People of color versus White people. And when you make a choice—for example, to plow highways first and clear sidewalks last—you're choosing to put one group before the other. How do your choices reflect your commitment to equity?

And keep in mind that there's a chicken-and-egg relationship between this "us versus them" mentality and inequity. When communities are stuck in "us versus them" framing, it naturally leads to inequity (after all, why would you treat "them" as equals?). And when there's inequity, people are more likely to see themselves as different from others in their community. It's a cycle.

You're Already Connected

When you're on the Buffalo Niagara Medical Campus (BNMC), if you look across Michigan Avenue to the east you'll see the Fruit Belt neighborhood. Across Main Street to the west is the Allentown neighborhood.

In our master plan, we don't refer to these streets as borders; instead, we call them seams. It's a deliberate choice of words that reflects how we see ourselves within the community—and, we hope, how our neighbors see us. Borders are designed to keep people on one side or the other. Seams, on the other hand, reflect the view that we are simply part of the fabric of the community.

"Instead of hard spatial geographies, where do you create porous open opportunities?" asked Tom Osha, board chair of The Global Institute on Innovation Districts, and senior vice president at Wexford Science & Technology. "The lines should be blurred." Unfortunately, we haven't always done this in Buffalo. As you walk around campus, it's clear that the layout and architecture often create artificial barriers between the institutions and the community. Although we can blame the fact that many of our buildings were constructed before the campus existed, we certainly have an opportunity to do better.

As I wrote in the Introduction, anchor institutions are so named in part because they don't typically move. They are anchored to the community, and the community is anchored to them. Being intertwined provides opportunities for everyone involved, such as a dance class for children in the community, taught by performing arts students at a university.

What some people fail to understand is that the issues that affect our community are also interrelated and that you can't fix one problem while ignoring others. If you want to end homelessness, you have to address healthcare. If you want to improve food security, you'd better think about public transportation. These issues are not simply interconnected; there is often a cause-and-effect relationship between them. For example, inequitable public transit limits access to polling locations. Limited access to polls leads to underrepresentation, which can lead to inadequate funding and support, causing the equity gaps to grow even wider. At its worst, this becomes a never-ending spiral. And yes, systemic issues are often significant contributors and root causes.

The COVID-19 pandemic further illustrated the extent to which we depend on each other. From schools and clinics to factories and grocery stores, essential workers risked (and lost) their lives providing vital goods and services to the public. People recognized these newly discovered connections, taping "Thank you, healthcare heroes" signs in their windows, wearing masks to protect others, and even stocking refrigerators on sidewalks with free vegetables for those in need.[3] On a more somber note, COVID-19 highlighted the ways in which inequities build upon themselves, as we saw more deaths from COVID-19 among Black people, people who live in cities with more air pollution, and the homeless, among other groups.

Improving equity can also provide benefits to people throughout the community—not just those who are underserved. This obviously isn't the point of improving equity; the goal, of course, is to help those who are marginalized. But in doing so, recognize that there may be additional positive outcomes for other groups. For example, creating a safer, more reliable public transit network improves the daily commute for employees who work nonstandard shifts and also serves people traveling into the city to go shopping or watch a show. "If I take a building and turn half of it into workforce training, I don't care if those folks who are trained end up working in the innovation district—I care about them working in the region," said Sam Fiorello, president and CEO of Cortex Innovation Community in St. Louis. "You can't just drive to the suburbs and think this doesn't affect me, because it does."

Talking about "us" doesn't mean treating everyone equally and providing everyone with the same solution—it means working to achieve equity. Think back to those kids trying to look over the fence. They don't all need the same height step stool—but they all need to be able to watch the game.

When we advance equity, everyone benefits, even if we all don't get the same thing. As the Utah Transit Authority stated in a campaign touting the benefits of public transit, "Even if you don't ride it, you use it."[4] Think about these types of shared goals that will benefit everyone in the community, even if they don't benefit everyone in the same way.

What problems can you solve that will help different groups of people? (And if you're not aware of the top community needs or what obstacles are in the way, refer back to chapter 2 and the social design process.)

Beyond Economic Impact

As you're prioritizing the community, consider the concept of use value versus exchange value. In a nutshell, the use value is what a resource is worth to the person who is using it, and the exchange value is what it's worth to someone else.[5] You can determine the exchange value of someone's house by asking the assessor's office. But if you want to know the use value, you have to talk with the homeowner or renter. When there's a wide discrepancy between use value and exchange value, you may find more tension. (You'll read more about this in chapter 10, where we talk about negotiating with homeowners.)

Another economic concept to keep in mind is a free good, which is something widely and (nearly) freely available. For example, drivers pay only a fraction of the real cost of driving. But what if the full cost weren't subsidized by cities, which build and maintain the roads that are often used by only a fraction of their residents? What if drivers had to pay not only for roads but the hospital bills of asthmatic patients and others affected by air pollution? If you are going to consider the economic cost, think about who is (and who isn't) bearing those costs.

People Have to Feel that They Belong

Who belongs in your anchor institution or innovation district? Who does an anchor institution or innovation district belong to? Even if you've followed social design principles and engaged the community, "us" needs to include—and provide opportunities for—everyone. If your organization is just for the people who work there, or other select audiences, it's not really serving the full community.

As the head of an innovation district, I find it frustrating because I know that we have services and resources that would benefit people in the surrounding neighborhoods. All people have to do is walk into the Innovation Center and ask. But I think there's a reason most people in the neighborhoods haven't taken that step—perhaps because they don't trust us as outsiders who came into their neighborhood and moved into this building. And why would they? The Innovation Center doesn't look like a building that's open to the public. We don't have a big glass lobby. We don't have signs telling people what they'll find inside. We don't leave the doors open or have people outside the building inviting passers-by to come in. Before you blame the community for not participating in your programs, think about it from their perspective.

Remove Barriers to Entry

So, how do we change that? In many cases, if people aren't engaging with your organization, it's not because they don't want to; it's because they can't. That's one reason why the Cleveland Foundation is moving their offices from the thirteenth floor of a downtown building, "dropping themselves right in the middle of the redlining map of Cleveland," says Jeff Epstein, the director of the Cleveland Health-Tech Corridor. The new space will help "reknit" neighborhoods bisected by Chester Avenue, an "artificial boundary" that divides communities. (The foundation also included community members as part of the developer selection process, as part of an effort to ensure a welcoming facility that belongs to everyone.) In New York City, zoning codes encourage developers to create public plazas in exchange for the ability to add more stories. Here in Buffalo, we've literally torn down fences in the innovation district—including one that we didn't *actually* have permission to remove, but that's a story for another day.

Sometimes, the barriers are easy to see, like a fence or the lack of wheelchair ramp. Sometimes they're not, especially if you're not part of a group that's affected by them. In St. Louis, the Cortex innovation district completed an equity audit of various buildings, looking for physical attributes such as multilingual signs, mothers' rooms, and gender-neutral bathrooms. But they also recognized that barriers aren't always physical—which is why their equity audit included reviewing things like the code of conduct within the district. In California, the Los Angeles Cleantech Incubator made Juneteenth a paid holiday for all employees. One of our member institutions, Kaleida Health, was recognized by the Human Rights Campaign Foundation for equitable treatment and inclusion of LGBTQ patients, visitors, and employees.

Don't just look at how you're serving people; consider how you're penalizing them, too. The CROWN Act—a law passed in more than a dozen municipalities from Covington, Kentucky, to Albuquerque, New Mexico—helps protect people from discrimination based on race-based hairstyles including braids and twists. In Columbus, Ohio, and numerous other cities, the library system has eliminated overdue book fines in an effort to promote knowledge and access.

What would happen if you went through your manuals and policies (and all the unofficial rules you enforce) and looked for ways to make everyone feel like they truly belong?

Open versus Welcome

Most years, we hold a STEM open house in the innovation district, inviting middle school and high school students to visit the facilities on campus and scrub into a simulated surgery, work alongside lab technicians, tour an active research laboratory, and much more.

It's easy to say, "Well, we opened our doors—what more can we do?"

But there's a difference between opening the doors and welcoming people in such a way they truly feel that they belong. Perhaps we should be more like the Pittsburgh Parks Conservancy, which placed "All Are Welcome" signs in its parks as part of their equity-focused initiatives. (And yes, if you're talking about "inviting" people in to your anchor institution or innovation district, it implies that they need an invitation. How can you change that?)

One thing we've done for key community-based programs is ensure that the facilitators look like the community we are a part of and serve. "It is vital to see women and people of color leading, and in positions as experts," explains Kyria Stephens, the BNMC director of inclusion and community initiatives. After all, if the person at the front of the room doesn't look like you, how does that make you feel? Although representation is important, it's only one of the reasons we asked women and people of color to lead our business academy classes. We thought that these instructors would be more effective at bringing in people from the surrounding community, especially those who hadn't attended any of our programs before. But most importantly, we knew that women and people of color could do a better job at teaching other women and people of color how to achieve success and overcome the obstacles they face. We didn't choose a diverse group of teachers because they were diverse; we chose them because we thought they would be the most effective in helping other women and people of color build and grow their businesses.

Innovation districts and anchor institutions can also help welcome people into the broader community. In Boston, the MASCO (the Medical Academic and Scientific Community Organization) innovation district worked with surrounding neighborhoods to create a website showcasing the area. Now, when you visit the website LongwoodArea .org, you can find walking tours, restaurants, and plenty of other things to do. The institutions all have comprehensive websites—why shouldn't the community?

What's Stopping You?

If you're not prioritizing what's best for the community, think about preconceptions and beliefs that may be holding you back.

In *Walkable City Rules*, Jeff Speck writes about the Housing First movement, which provides long-term housing for people experiencing homelessness. As Speck documents, the movement has been proven to reduce homelessness, lower the number of emergency room visits, and save cities tens of thousands of dollars a year for each person who participates. Yet many cities still don't participate, in part because some people still see homelessness as a punishment of sorts. "Are you really willing to spend twice as much on homelessness, and have twice as much of it," writes Speck, "because you believe that people should be punished for addiction and mental illness?"[6]

If you think that people in your community *deserve* to be homeless (or poor, hungry, etc.), then you're unlikely to put their needs first. As you face "us versus them" thinking, consider the underlying beliefs that drive these divisions.

When There Is a "Them"

Although I advocate for breaking down the "us versus them" mentality within communities, I do think you should be wary of those outside your community, at least until they've proven that they have your city's best interests at heart.

A few years ago, 238 cities sent Amazon a proposal, trying to convince the online giant to build a new headquarters in their city and bring in tens of thousands of jobs. Long Island City in Queens was one of the winners. And then they said, "No, thanks."

Despite the global appeal of Amazon, Queens rejected it, said urban planner Alex Krieger, "because they felt benefits would accrue only one way. There was no assurance that housing costs wouldn't splurge much higher, that jobs would go to people living in Queens, and so forth." (Of course, it's not just about jobs; with any new development, a community needs to be able to support the increase in traffic, energy requirements, schools for employees' children, and more.)

Is your community putting resources toward the existing residents ("us") or outsiders ("them")? If you'll offer tax breaks to strangers, why not do the same for your friends? What if, instead of incentivizing outside companies to come to their communities, cities and innovation districts invested more in the people who were already there?

Language Matters

What you say—and how you say it—reflects your priorities. As one city planner explained, we should avoid using words like *pedestrian* and instead refer to people who walk. After all, we are all people first, and should not be defined by our mode of transportation on any given day.[7] Here in Buffalo, our innovation district published a pledge for racial equity, and we're inspired by cities like Spartanburg, South Carolina, where the City Council passed a resolution that acknowledges systemic racism and apologizes for injustices and inequities.[8] Former Buffalo-based broadcast journalist and anchor Madison Carter successfully advocated for numerous antiracist policies, including the use of specific neighborhood names rather than grouping multiple areas together as the "East Side," which isn't a neighborhood but rather a collection of communities where Black people live.[9]

Pay attention to the order of your words, too. As David Gamble recalls, when we unveiled the master plan for our innovation district to various groups, we quickly realized that the first slides in our presentation were geared toward the institutions—not the communities. When we were talking to neighborhoods, we needed to start by focusing on what was important to them—even if the overall content was the same.

Visualization tools can also improve equity by making data more accessible, which not only allows more people to understand the data but also often makes it easier for everyone to see how inequities appear in their community. Los Angeles, for example, uses an Equity Index to map "disparities and barriers to opportunity" in more than one hundred neighborhoods.[10]

Actions Speak Louder than Words

What you say is important, but what you do is even more so.

As you're thinking about your actions, ask yourself: Does your budget reflect the community's priorities? Does the way you spend and receive money promote equity? For example, one study from Richmond, Virginia, showed that public defenders were paid significantly less than prosecutors. How would equity be improved if public defenders were paid the same, leading to more experienced attorneys staying in those positions? What's the equivalent in your organization? What are you valuing and rewarding (or undervaluing) with how you spend money? Does your budget reflect an "us versus them" mentality?

Recently, we've seen many communities demand more input into how their tax dollars are being spent, including requests to spend less on law enforcement and more on proactive social services. In Philadelphia, for example, there's a proposal to let residents share ideas and vote on how a $1 million budget will be allocated (still a tiny fraction of the city's $4.5 billion overall budget, but it's a start.) The city also plans to further explore how departments must consider how budget changes may affect racial disparities.[11]

Some organizations are also establishing specific racial equity funds. Although I applaud the intention, I caution you not to put all of the burden for equity-related initiatives on a single fund or office. Establishing separate departments and overseers, though well intentioned, should not shift the responsibility to promote equity from everyone in the organization to the select few "in charge" of it. Promoting equity should be an organization-wide imperative, perhaps led by experts in creating equitable communities.

Consistency matters. "You have to continue to show up," explains Beth Machnica, the director of community well-being for the BNMC. Machnica spends a significant amount of her time working directly with people in the surrounding neighborhoods. She sees firsthand the mistrust that exists between the community and anchor institutions. And she knows that there's often skepticism about the organization's motivations and how committed we are to truly putting the community's needs first. "You have to show people that you're not just checking a box for a grant," she says. "You need to prove that your project isn't just a touchpoint."

Especially in the beginning days of the BNMC, I would go out in the community and ask what we could do to help. I remember going with the chairman of our board, with rakes in hand, to help with their fall cleanup on a crisp Saturday morning. We showed up—not because we had to, but because we see our role as serving the community.

We are us.

CHAPTER 7
Steal Shamelessly

My favorite football team is the Buffalo Bills. For me, there's no other team like them.

Except there are, in fact, dozens of other teams in the National Football League. They may have different players and wear different uniforms, but they're all trying to achieve the same purpose: win games.

It's the same thing with cities. Your city is unique. It's filled with people and places you won't find anywhere else in the world. But in more ways than not, your city is the same as hundreds of cities around the world.

You have streets and sidewalks. You have companies and utilities, schools and nonprofits. You have more challenges than you have hours in the day. You have opportunities to serve your community and, hopefully, close the equity gap. You have some solutions that are working—and others that still need work.

Your city is special, but it's not that special.

The good news is, this means you don't have to solve every problem yourself. Chances are, other cities have found solutions to the same types of challenges you're dealing with right now. You don't have to waste your time reinventing the wheel. It's a lot more efficient to see what other cities are already doing, then implement their proven ideas in your community.

The effectiveness of this approach was made crystal clear to us during a breakfast meeting with a senior international business executive. "He pointed out that what we were doing was hardly unique—it wasn't rocket science," recalls Thomas Beecher Jr., who was chairman of our campus at that time. "There were many successful examples of medical campuses around the country. He said we should see what other campuses had done and how they accomplished it, and then do what he had done to build his business—steal ideas shamelessly from the competition and put them to work in Buffalo."

Steal shamelessly. We do it. Steve Jobs did it ("we have always been shameless about stealing great ideas").[1] And if you aren't doing it already, it's time to start.

In this chapter, we'll talk about stealing ideas that can help you close the equity gap. We'll see how you can glean inspiration from other cities, other industries, other countries, and your partners. And we'll discuss how to take what you've learned and apply it to your organization.

Steal from Other Anchor Institutions and Innovation Districts

If you're going to steal ideas, the natural place to start is by looking at other anchor institutions and innovation districts. They're most likely to be facing challenges and opportunities similar to the ones on your to-do list.

But with dozens of innovation districts in the United States alone (not to mention thousands of anchor institutions), where do you start?

It's common sense, but you really do get the most out of visiting your peers. If you're building an innovation district in Miami, you're probably not going to get much out of visiting the Peoria Innovation District in Illinois. Find the cities that are similar to yours—in terms of size, certainly, but also in terms of your city's demographics, primary industries, and other key factors. Ideally, you want to study anchors and innovation districts that have dealt with the same challenges you're facing, which usually means they're at the same stage of growth as you are, or perhaps a few years ahead of you.

When we started the medical campus in Buffalo, we took trips to campuses in Houston and Milwaukee. We also visited Johns Hopkins and Cleveland Clinic, even though we knew we might never be in their league. Why? Because we wanted to be inspired. I knew as a teenager that I would never play basketball as well as Michael Jordan, but I could still learn something by watching his games. If we had skipped these trips, we would have missed out on dozens of ideas. Going to some of the best medical campuses in the world showed us what was possible, even if those possibilities were decades away. Make sure you have at least one aspirational, best-in-class institution on your list.

Where to Go, What to Ask

If you're on a tight budget, you can still learn a lot about other cities through phone calls with your counterparts in other communities. You can even ask someone to take you on a virtual tour with their smartphone. Joining industry groups and attending conferences can also provide inspiration and ideas at a minimal cost. Since launching the Buffalo Niagara Medical Campus (BNMC), we have gained invaluable insights and advice through groups such as the BIO International Convention, InBIA, and the Association of University Research Parks—and we continue to learn through these and other leading organizations, including the Anchor District Council and The Global Institute on Innovation Districts.

If your budget and schedule allow, you really need to visit cities in person. Spending a few days in a city lets you feel what it's really like—how people ebb and flow throughout the streets. It also gives your hosts a chance to let their guard down and go beyond the typical guided tour and talking points. The "a-ha" moments don't usually appear on a PowerPoint slide; they happen while you're walking to dinner or hanging out at the local coffee shop.

We visited half a dozen innovation districts when we were starting the BNMC, which was enough to learn a lot without getting overwhelmed. But we probably would have been better off visiting only three or four at the beginning and then going to a few more once we had been in operation for a year or two.

One of the best decisions we made was to bring a sizable contingent on some of our pivotal fact-finding trips. Our trip to Louisville, for example, included Buffalo's mayor, the Common Council president, a newspaper reporter, and representatives from our board, Buffalo's leading economic development organization, and a local foundation that supported our work. But by the time we flew back to Buffalo, we had, quite literally, a plane full of ambassadors for our new innovation district, all of whom had seen what Buffalo could become. "It opened people's eyes because it created an opportunity for us to see firsthand the wow factor—you know, 'Man, this can work! We can all do this together,'" recalls former Buffalo mayor and critical partner Tony Masiello. "By visiting other cities, we learned from them the 'good, bad, and ugly' of their operations and relationships, which helped us eliminate the 'ugly.'"

Bringing key stakeholders also lets them meet their counterparts and understand what role they may—or may not—want to play back home. "In some cities, like Louisville, the mayor himself was going to be the driving force of the unification of the investment of the medical campus there," says Masiello. "It was very clear to me that it was better for me to put the team together of people who know what they were doing and how to do it, then get out of their way and give them the support and encouragement and whatever city resources they needed to make this thing successful."

Looking back, I know we should have invited more people from our community (specifically those from marginalized groups) to take the trip to Louisville and other cities with us—not just elected officials and business leaders. Other people might have asked more questions about affordable housing and public transportation, pointed out areas where these cities fell short in serving the community, and, not inconsequentially, helped us share the message about Buffalo's medical campus throughout their neighborhoods. This was truly one of our biggest mistakes, leaving out some of the most important people in the process. So why did we do it? We didn't intentionally exclude them. Equity simply wasn't at the forefront when we took some of these trips, when we were first starting the innovation district. Fortunately, we've learned from our mistakes—and I hope you will too.

Deep in the Heart

Our first major benchmarking trip was to the Texas Medical Center in Houston. David Hohn (president and CEO of Buffalo's Roswell Park Comprehensive Cancer Center at the time) had come from Houston and arranged for a number of us to embark on an extensive, all-day tour of the campus. As Hohn recalls, the executive director of Texas Medical Center was married to a woman who was from Buffalo and had received life-saving cancer treatment at Roswell Park as a child, so they rolled out the red carpet for us. The only payment he asked for was a big box of Ted's Hot Dogs (a local favorite), which we shipped to him after our trip.

Everything really is bigger in Texas, and it was truly an eye-opening experience to get a behind-the-scenes look at the world's largest medical complex. One of the most valuable ideas we stole from Texas was the idea of "collabo-tition," with competing institutions working together toward common objectives. As we discussed in chapter 4, this concept laid the groundwork for our Table of Trust. But it was a more practical discovery that helped us quickly gain solid financial footing in Buffalo. "One of the biggest lessons we learned," noted Thomas Beecher Jr., "was that the entire budget for the campus operation of over $40 million was paid for by control of parking on the Texas Medical Center campus." Like Texas, we weren't aiming to maximize revenues but rather to serve our member institutions and the community, which still requires significant funding. So we quickly (and successfully) applied the Texas model in Buffalo, and we continue to fund many of our operations through parking revenue today, even as we look for new ideas to replace parking revenue with the anticipated rise of autonomous vehicles.

We're far from the only innovation district that gets ideas from our peers, of course. Representatives from St. Louis visited Kendall Square when they were planning the city's Cortex Innovation Community.[2] Every year, we typically host hundreds of representatives from other districts here in Buffalo. If I surveyed my peers, I'd guess that most of them have visited at least one other innovation district in the past year. Of course, we continue to visit other anchor institutions and innovation districts on a regular basis.

Visits aren't just for stealing ideas, of course. They're an opportunity to build relationships, grow your network, and—hopefully—confirm that you're already on the right track. As business leaders considering an innovation district in Phoenix wrote after their visit to Buffalo, "the greatest takeaway business and political leaders got from this trip is that we already have all many of the necessary pieces to form a cohesive, world class medical destination."[3]

Now, a quick aside: I understand that the word "steal" has negative connotations and may turn some people off. I use it more tongue-in-cheek, as a reminder of the recommendation to "steal shamelessly." But there are lots of other ways to describe this concept. For example, "benchmarking" definitely sounds more civil than "stealing." After all, nobody ever said, "Thou shalt not benchmark." So call it what you will—stealing, benchmarking, borrowing, fact-finding—it's the same basic premise; you're looking to others for inspiration and ideas. And keep in mind that many organizations, like ours, are more than willing to share what they've learned. Some (especially forward-thinking governments and grassroots groups) even post their manuals and plans online and encourage others to copy their process. As you find solutions to creating a more equitable city, I'd urge you to be generous with your time and resources and help others who are building more equitable communities.

Steal from Other Cities

Other innovation districts may have the most applicable ideas, but they certainly shouldn't be your sole source of inspiration. You need to broaden your horizons—sometimes literally—to discover the best ideas.

It's a twenty-one-hour trip from Cleveland to Curitiba, Brazil, including a few layovers. But it was worth every minute for representatives from Cleveland's University Circle innovation district, who wanted to see firsthand how Brazil's bus rapid transit (BRT) system could make public transit more accessible and reduce greenhouse gas emissions. BRT uses designated lanes, prioritized signals, and stations—like rail, but with the flexibility of buses.

"The delegation came back with the notion that we could create a simulated rail system that would be about ten percent of the cost of a fixed rail system," noted Chris Ronayne, president of University Circle. Inspired by the Brazilians, Cleveland built a BRT line between downtown and the University Circle anchor district. Named HealthLine in honor of the hospitals that help maintain the stations, the BRT slashed commute times by nearly one third, provided the highest return on investment of any public transit project in the United States ($9.5 billion), and addresses climate change with hybrid electric buses that reduce emissions by 90 percent.[4]

Beyond making transportation more accessible and sustainable, other cities—especially more progressive ones—are constantly developing and evolving initiatives designed specifically to address equity-related issues. In Seattle, for example, "all public health department staff must participate in a two-day training on institutionalized racism."[5] Nationwide, cities from Nashville to San Antonio are hiring chief equity officers. Many community-wide equity efforts are still focused primarily on racism, but others are going beyond, addressing issues such as income inequality, sexism, and individual bias. (Buffalo recently began providing diversity and inclusion training to all city employees, beginning with the fire department.)

What would happen if everyone in your organization was trained in how to recognize and address institutional racism? Why not take it a step (or two) further? What if every employee of every anchor institution in your city offered training? What if every developer had to train their crew before breaking ground on any new construction projects? How would these practices improve equity in your city?

I know what you're thinking: We could never do that here because, well, every community has its reasons. I have the same thought every time I hear ideas that might make people uncomfortable. But remember that you're not alone. People in Seattle are having uncomfortable conversations about race, too. When you steal an idea, you're also stealing the time-tested process that goes with it. And when you run into resistance (and you will), you can point to the fact that someone else already did it successfully, which is an excellent way to quiet the critics.

Start at Home

Sometimes, the best ideas are closer than you think. When the University of Pennsylvania and other organizations banded together to form the University City District, they based it on Philadelphia's Center City District, only a few miles away. Looking to other areas of your city for inspiration lets you start from a familiar place and offers at least some reassurance that your initiative can work in your community.

If you're part of an innovation district or other network, it's worth noting the resources your member institutions may have to offer. When we started the BNMC we needed a logo, but we didn't have any graphic designers on staff. I found out that one of our hospital partners employed a designer, so I asked him to design a logo for us. It's a bit different today; we have a few dozen people on our staff, but even now, if there's something I need that's outside our expertise, I don't hesitate to pick up the phone and ask our partners if we can steal some of their time. We've also formalized these interinstitutional relationships through work councils, which bring together people in similar roles from across organizations. Each month, our director of communications meets with other communications directors, our transportation manager meets with other transportation managers, and so on.

Look Around

As Yogi Berra said, "You can observe a lot by watching."[6] And the more you observe, the more hidden clues you may find in your quest to promote equity. Consider an anecdote from Jane Jacobs's landmark work *The Death and Life of Great American Cities*, in which she describes what she learned from a simple newspaper ad for a chain of bookstores with locations throughout the city.

In most boroughs, according to the ad Jacobs read, the local store was open until midnight. But the Brooklyn location closed at 8 p.m. "Here is a management which keeps its stores open late, if there is business to be had. The advertisement tells us that Brooklyn's downtown is too dead by 8 p.m., as indeed it is. No surveys (and certainly no mindless, mechanical predictions projected forward in time from statistical surveys, a boondoggle that today frequently passes for 'planning') can tell us anything so relevant to the composition and to the need of Brooklyn's downtown as this small, but specific and precisely accurate, clue to the workings of that downtown."[7]

Things have changed in recent years. Today, we look online for a bookstore's hours, not in the newspaper. And a quick scan confirms that many Brooklyn bookstores are open just as late as (if not later than) their Manhattan counterparts. So what is there to steal here? How does knowing that a bookstore closes at 8 p.m. help you create a more equitable city?

The hours are simply a data point for you to interpret. Even if Jacobs was right, and downtown really was "too dead," you need to understand why before you can act. Maybe the bookstore is in a business district, where everyone goes home at 6 p.m. Maybe it's in a residential neighborhood, but it's not safe to be outside after dark. Maybe it *is* safe, but the residents don't think it is. Or maybe Jacobs was wrong, and the bookstore specialized in Eastern European literature in a neighborhood filled with South Asian immigrant families, so they closed up early. Each of these findings leads to a different plan of action, but you won't know for sure until you dig deeper. Only then can you use what you've learned about the bookstore—and hence, about the community—to address inequities.

These days, of course, it's easy to "look around" without ever leaving your desk or favorite coffee shop. In five minutes, you can get more data on your smartphone than you could from spending a day at the library thirty years ago. But staring at your phone (or hunkering down in the library) will never give you the full story. As Eric Klinenberg wrote in *Palaces for the People*, "Statistics do not convey the differences between poor, minority neighborhoods that are cursed with empty lots, broken sidewalks, abandoned homes, and shuttered storefronts, and those that are densely peopled, busy with foot traffic, enlivened by commercial activity and well-maintained parks, and supported by strong community organizations."[8]

Back in graduate school, we learned about MBWA—management by walking around—the idea that you could keep your finger on the pulse of an organization by roaming the halls and talking to employees. Now, I prefer to think of it as BBWA—borrowing by walking around. Turn off your phone and go take a walk. You won't regret it.

And when you do turn your phone back on, spend a minute thinking about the digital tools that are changing the way individuals and organizations achieve results. Take crowdfunding, which is being used to raise billions of dollars each year. Instead of a campaign to help launch a new product or pay someone's medical bills, consider how you could use crowdsourcing to promote equity on a city-wide scale. My point isn't to focus on crowdsourcing specifically (although you probably should) but to open your eyes to all the other tools out there.

Read the Research

Anchor institutions such as universities and medical centers are filled with people studying nearly every imaginable topic. Although you probably don't need to know about quantum mechanics or the mating habits of ducks, there are hundreds, perhaps thousands of research areas that directly or indirectly apply to equitable cities.

Here's an example: Research shows that, with cars readily available, "North Americans will walk only if it is easier than driving. The breakpoint for walking trips seems to be five minutes, which is enough time to walk approximately one quarter mile, or four hundred meters."[9]

Once you know this fact about human behavior, you can use it to create more equitable communities. Let's say you're trying to improve health and fight climate change by reducing the number of miles that people drive in your city. How can you reduce distances to the most frequented destinations for underserved residents? Better yet, how can you incentivize people to walk more than five minutes?

Another steal-worthy concept is risk homeostasis, a fancy term that simply describes "how people automatically adjust their behavior to maintain a comfortable level of risk."[10] If your goal is to reduce the number of pedestrian deaths in your community—and you understand risk homeostasis—you may notice a surprising commonality among the deadliest intersections in your city; they're "typically the ones you can navigate with one finger on the steering wheel and a cellphone at your ear."[11] Of course, you might come to this same conclusion even if you've never heard of risk homeostasis, but learning about this aspect of human behavior enables you to understand *why* these intersections are more dangerous, so you can create more effective solutions and avoid similar mistakes in the future.

Just as my trip to Texas inspired me to try "collabo-tition" here, stealing ideas from outside your typical environment lets you discover creative solutions to the challenges in your community. In Sweden, officials are gamifying driving habits; drivers who stay under the speed limit can "win a percentage of the speeding ticket revenues, every week!"[12] Planners at the United Nations use the Minecraft video game to let people visualize public spaces.[13] It doesn't matter where the ideas come from, whether it's from the *Journal of Behavioral and Experimental Economics*, your daughter's video game, or something you saw on the bulletin board at your local library. The point is simple: Open your eyes to everything around you, and be ready to steal.

Know What Not to Steal

When I take people on tours of our campus, one of our first stops is the parking lot across the street, where I tell people to look up and see one of our most expensive mistakes: wind- and solar-powered street lights. It was a good plan, in theory; each lamp would be powered by a 5-foot-tall vertical wind turbine and a photovoltaic panel, with electricity stored in a lithium ion battery in the base of each pole. "Once installed," we proudly proclaimed on our website, "these lamps will no longer be tied into the electrical grid."

Except they failed. Within two years, they all stopped working. I won't bore you with the technical details here; instead, I'll just encourage you to steal from others' failures—not just their successes—which is why it's important to make sure you're helping to set the agenda when you're talking with your peers in another city. You don't want just the highlight tour. You're not a convention planner who needs to be wined and dined. You're there because you have challenges in your city, and you want to learn how to solve them. Be honest, share your challenges, and tell your peers that you want to understand their approach to similar problems.[14] As our former chairman, Thomas Beecher Jr., noted, "the places we visited were very generous in sharing mistakes they had made so we could avoid them." These days, I try to pay it forward by sharing our mistakes with my peers throughout the country. That's not easy when you're speaking in front of two thousand people at a conference, but it's the right thing to do. When representatives from other cities come to Buffalo, I like to take them on a walking tour of our campus (starting with the infamous parking lot lights) *and* the surrounding areas, including one of the poorest neighborhoods in the city. I make sure we have plenty of time to stop and talk with the people who live and work here. And I don't sugarcoat the fact that we still have a long way to go.

You Be You

"Be yourself. Everyone else is already taken." It's one of my favorite quotes, often attributed (probably mistakenly) to Oscar Wilde. Regardless of who said it, the sentiment remains true. You can't be something that you're not. I started this chapter by telling you that your city isn't really that different. But it's also true that no two cities are identical. Every city has its own patterns, its own potential, its own flaws.

When we created the medical campus in Buffalo, we started by focusing on our strengths and leveraging the resources we already had. In a letter from 2000 inviting key institutions to join us, our chairman wrote, "We boast the number nine cancer institute in the country, a Nobel laureate at Hauptman-Woodward, a major cardiac center at the Buffalo General, the center of U.B.'s medical teaching, and, hopefully, to be joined by the 19th children's hospital in the country." As we noted in our master plan, we weren't "building anything from scratch" but rather "taking what is there and strengthening it."

Your city has a history. A legacy. Points of pride that can form the foundation for a more equitable future. We see it in cities like Detroit— where the automotive industry was born—now (smartly) focused on *equitable* mobility, with work showcased in the Cooper Hewitt, Smithsonian Design Museum.[15] You have to be yourself. You can't just copy what others are doing and expect success. Every time I travel I'm looking for great ideas and thinking about how (or whether) we can "Buffalo-ize" it. I don't want to squash creative thinking, but you can't see something in New York City and automatically say you're going to do it in Buffalo. We simply don't have the population to support some of their best ideas. Other differences matter, too. You can be inspired by Seattle's diversity training program, for example, but if you try the same exact thing in San Antonio it probably won't be as effective. Yes, both cities have racial inequities, but the *types* of inequities differ in countless ways because of differences in demographics, cultural history, and countless other factors. Granted, if you see the same idea implemented successfully in multiple cities, there may be a greater chance that it will work for you, too. But don't count on it. "Merely mimicking a successful project is perilous because it's difficult to ascertain the social, economic, political, and physical context in which the project takes place."[16]

A whiteboard full of ideas might look impressive in your office, but it's useless if they aren't right for your city. Go ahead and steal shamelessly; just make sure you credit whoever you're stealing from (especially if it's someone from a marginalized community, whose ideas are often stolen without proper recognition), and think carefully about how the ideas will work in your community.

CHAPTER 8
Listen to the Visionaries

Larry Jacobs didn't want to go into the family business. Back in 1915, his father had started a company selling popcorn and peanuts to sports teams and theaters. The business was doing well, but Larry had always wanted to be a doctor, ever since he visited a hospital as a kid and was drawn in by the sights, sounds, and smells of the busy hallways.

As his brother took over the family business and grew it into one of the top hospitality companies in the world, Larry happily went to medical school and enjoyed a rewarding career as a clinician and researcher.

At one point, when Larry was consulting for a cancer institute, he wondered whether one of the drugs they were testing for cancer therapy could alleviate symptoms for his patients with multiple sclerosis.

He applied for funding from the National Institutes of Health, which turned him down. But he believed in his vision, so he raised money from local businesses and philanthropists to fund his research privately. That research led to the development of Avonex, which became the most widely prescribed drug for patients with relapsing multiple sclerosis.

Larry was a visionary. And when he passed away from cancer at age sixty-three, we lost a man who not only cared deeply about his patients but also had the foresight and persistence to make a difference for hundreds of thousands of people around the world.[1]

Visionaries challenge the status quo. They're not content with the way things are. In this chapter we'll talk about who they are, how to work with them, and how they can help you advance equity.

In Every Community

Anchor institutions and innovation districts, by their nature, often attract forward-thinking people. But they're hardly the only places you'll find visionaries. People who are ahead of their time can be found everywhere, whether they're a scientist running a research lab, a resident who lives in the surrounding neighborhood, or an elected official who sits on the city council. They're in governments and nonprofits. Startups and block clubs. You just have to look for them. I've met visionaries who work for five-person companies and others who run five-thousand-person organizations.

Here in Buffalo, we're lucky to have visionaries such as Samina Raja, who founded one of the first "food labs" in the country and helped bring mobile gardens, farmers' markets, and food trucks to food deserts throughout the city. I think of people like former Buffalo mayor Tony Masiello, who could often be seen pulling a small speaker and microphone system around the neighborhood before the Buffalo Niagara Medical Campus (BNMC) became a reality, talking to anyone who would listen about what would be there someday. "'We were selling hope at the start,'" he said in an interview with *The Buffalo News*.[2] In the beginning, you may not have much more than hope and a vision. But that's okay. Keep going. You may not achieve your vision—but you surely won't if you simply give up.

And then there's attorney Al Mugel. Long before the BNMC came to fruition in 2001, Al helped lead efforts to establish a medical campus in

Buffalo. The community wasn't ready at the time, but Mugel was undeterred and kept advocating for his vision. Years later, when we refined Mugel's plans and started getting local leaders on board, he became one of our staunchest advocates and most loyal partners. (He had also established a corporate structure for the original entity and kept up with the annual filing requirements, so when the BNMC was officially established, all we had to do was change the name on the paperwork.)

Sometimes, a visionary is just someone who can see the success of one community and apply it to others—something to keep in mind if you're in a city that isn't typically at the forefront. Elizabeth "Betty" Capaldi Phillips, former provost at the University at Buffalo, set a high bar for success. Phillips arrived here from Gainesville, Florida, where the invention of Gatorade at the University of Florida brought in hundreds of millions of dollars in royalties. That was her benchmark. In less than a decade in Buffalo, Phillips helped increase UB's footprint on the medical campus more than twenty-fold, thanks in large part to her tireless efforts and extraordinary vision.

Buffalo Medical Group traces its origins to World War II, when a doctor in the U.S. Army Medical Corps learned about a new, more effective way to provide care. Instead of treating patients alone—a common practice at the time—he started working together with other doctors to save soldiers' lives. When the war ended, this doctor joined three others with similar experiences to start the practice, now one of the largest of its kind in New York State. Remember the lessons about "stealing shamelessly" from chapter 7, look for visionaries who can translate successes from other areas, and replicate them in your community.

When people think of visionaries, they often picture someone sitting at the head of the table or speaking at the front of the room. But visionaries aren't always in leadership roles. In fact, most of the true visionaries I've met tend to take on leadership positions reluctantly, if at all. As a result, visionaries may be harder to identify (because they're often further down the org chart) and may not have the authority of a C-level leader to act on their vision. Which means that if you're in a position of power, you can help recognize and amplify ideas from visionaries, regardless of their status within an organization.

A Vision of a Better World

Visionaries often play a significant role in addressing inequities. Years ago, Rosanne Haggerty founded a group that created affordable housing for thousands of people in New York City. But she realized that these homes didn't address the systemic issues that drive rising homelessness. So she started thinking about the problem differently. Now, as president of Community Solutions and architect of its "Built for Zero" initiative, she has helped more than a dozen communities (and counting) achieve what she calls "functional zero" in terms of veteran or chronic homelessness. Her approach fundamentally changes how communities address homelessness by acknowledging that you don't necessarily need more resources to tackle the problem; you need a different mindset. You need to stop thinking that those experiencing homelessness are to blame, don't want help, or will have all their problems solved through affordable housing. Instead, Haggerty's plan relies on building partnerships, integrating efforts, and studying data. Specifically, it tracks the needs of each person experiencing homelessness, the number of people, and how this number changes over time. "Using this data," the organization explains, "communities are better [able] to triage the needs of every individual in need of support, implement and test systems changes, target resources, and understand whether collective efforts are driving reductions in homelessness."[3] (This approach is also far less expensive than simply building new homes—further proof that listening to visionaries doesn't have to be costly.) In 2021, Community Solutions was awarded a $100-million grant from the MacArthur Foundation to continue working toward their vision and help cities throughout the United States end homelessness.

Pay Attention to What They're Saying

Larry Jacobs was trying to use a cancer drug to help patients with multiple sclerosis. Rosanne Haggerty decided to address homelessness without building more homes. When you first hear these ideas, they seem a little bizarre. People prefer the status quo. As you may recall from chapter 1, when we first talked to people about getting competitors to work together, many people said it would never work.

Here's what I can tell you: Just keep pushing through. Visionaries don't give up. They believe in their vision. That doesn't mean you shouldn't question them. But don't dismiss them because of your first impression of them or their ideas.

When someone is opposed to a visionary idea, think about what they're really criticizing. People may be opposed to visionaries (and their ideas) because of implicit or explicit biases, which are far-too-common causes of inequity. Consider whether the critics are opposed to a visionary's ultimate goal or to their plan for achieving it. Often, I've found that critics are more focused on the process than the actual idea. You'll hear things like, "That will never work," or "That's not the way we do things."

For example, when we tried to create the BNMC, people didn't doubt that our community would be better if the competing hospitals worked together. They recognized the value of our goal. They just didn't think we could get it done, largely because it hadn't been done before. In my experience, that's a common objection to visionary ideas. But it's also a fairly weak argument that's usually easy to overcome. Remember the five whys exercise from chapter 2. Ask why, and keep asking why until you get to the real root of the issue.

Visionaries are focused on the future, not the past. The good news is, once you start making progress toward your vision, people are more likely to jump on board because, even if they don't fully agree with the process, they believe in the end result.

Share Their Vision

Look for opportunities to leverage the visionary's work by sharing them, and their vision, with other key stakeholders in the community. When urban planner Alex Krieger made his first visit to Buffalo to start thinking about a master plan for our innovation district, he gave us a few quick impressions after his first day here. He was going to spend the next day doing more sketching and touring before flying home and writing his full report, but our chairman at the time realized that Krieger's vision would be ten times more powerful if people could hear it firsthand. So we quickly put together a dinner for the next night and got as many people as we could in a room to hear Krieger's plans. It was clear to many of them that Krieger was a visionary who could see the future of the campus, which helped us tremendously in terms of gaining momentum and support from the community.

Recognize the value that visionaries can provide throughout your community. During our partnership with Health Care Without Harm, we brought one of their experts, Jennifer Obadia, to Buffalo a few times each year to provide guidance. But we also scheduled meetings for her to talk with anchor institutions, large nonprofits, and other organizations throughout the city. "We wanted the partnership to benefit the entire community, not just the medical campus," says Beth Machnica, our director of community well-being. These opportunities led to substantive changes, including one government agency realizing that they didn't have questions about food security on a health assessment and subsequently adjusting the survey to include questions that let us gather more data and advocate for change.

Adapt Their Vision to Your Community

We often find that visionaries who can have the most impact on our community are not even from our city. That said, although an outside perspective offers advantages, it's not always fully applicable.

For example, despite the best efforts of countless healthcare practitioners here in Buffalo, our community does not have a strong culture of health. Only 58 percent of residents said they went to their doctor routinely to check their blood pressure and cholesterol, compared with 75 percent of people nationwide.[4]

So when we have the chance to work with visionaries in health and wellness, we find that many of their ideas will work here in Buffalo, but some of them just won't. Other cities are often years ahead of us in terms of healthy eating practices and trends. As much as it pains us to do so, we often have to take small steps. "It's unrealistic, at least today, to say we want 100 percent of the people to be healthy 100 percent of the time," explains Machnica. You know your community best. As you listen to the visionaries, consider how you may need to adapt their vision to have a chance of it working in your city, as we discussed when talking about stealing shamelessly.

The Flaws of Visionaries

Visionaries aren't perfect. One person I've worked closely with was successful in bringing his vision to fruition but ran into problems when everyone else saw his success and wanted a piece of it. By that point, he was accustomed to working mostly by himself, and he bristled when others tried to get involved. He didn't communicate his plans well. He focused on what he thought were the priorities, perhaps at the expense of other community needs. And pretty soon, people started to resent the power he wielded throughout the neighborhood. Visionaries don't always realize that they need other people around them to help execute on their vision. This is an important point in terms of advancing equity, because you want to ensure that a visionary's work is truly serving the community and not just fulfilling their personal vision.

Different visionaries have different strengths. Some may be excellent at seeing the big picture and mapping out a holistic plan for an entire community. Others may work within a much more narrow range—for example, focusing on the future of accessible transportation or renewable energy or gender equality. Recognize and respect their scope.

Visionaries are great for figuring out where you're going, but someone has to do the everyday work of executing the strategic vision. Visionaries aren't usually the ones responsible for running the day-to-day operations, for good reason: They may be so focused on the future that they're not always paying enough attention to the present. Visionaries are important, but they probably shouldn't make up most (or even the majority) of your team.

Be a Visionary

You don't have to be a visionary to act like one. Visionaries are just people who see things sooner than the rest of us. And there's a fine line between being a visionary and simply being proactive, which is often nearly as good—and a lot easier to do.

Being proactive just means thinking about things as early as possible. Ask yourself, "What are the issues that we'll face tomorrow, a year from now, or a hundred years from now?" And then think about what you can do now to create more equitable communities in the future.

For example, many cities have taken a proactive approach to addressing common land management issues. In Greenville, South Carolina, the city kept ownership of land surrounding a park to help avoid (or at least mitigate) gentrification and displacement.[5] Land is typically much more affordable when you do this early in the planning stages.

You can look ahead and surmise that equitable restroom access may be a growing concern in the future. Or consider parking garages, many of which will probably need to be decommissioned when self-driving vehicles are the norm. If you're constructing a new building, having the vision to see these changes on the horizon may give you the opportunity to invest a bit more up front to future-proof your facility. For example, you may include all-gender restrooms in your plans or design a parking garage with built-in utilities, which makes it much easier to convert to apartments or offices.[6]

(This type of long-term thinking may be more familiar ground for anchor institutions than for innovation districts, given that many anchors have been in the community for decades and are accustomed to looking generations ahead. Innovation districts, on the other hand, are typically much newer organizations, without the history to draw upon.)

Looking far ahead helps ensure that you can have the greatest impact. In Philadelphia, Drexel University anticipates significant real estate development around the campus in the next twenty years, according to Lucy Kerman, senior vice provost. "Today, the families in our neighborhoods aren't getting those jobs," says Kerman. "They're not getting the entry-level job, the catering job, the marketing job, they're not even getting the job to provide the business cards for the businesses." Looking ahead to when those buildings are fully built out, Kerman is already anticipating what needs to happen to create an equitable community, from early childhood education and schools to healthcare and trauma support. "Our vision is that children born in the neighborhood today will be ready for those jobs."

Even if you're not able to act like a visionary, you can find ways to support them. We provide office space, access to experts, programming support, and other resources that help companies thrive. In fact, one of these companies—ACV Auctions, valued at nearly $4 billion after their IPO—is still headquartered in the BNMC Innovation Center. By

working closely with visionaries at large companies, individual entrepreneurs, and many in between, we can help build a more resilient city.

Pilots and Prototypes

One way to prove the feasibility of your vision is to test it through pilot
projects or prototypes. You can't test everything, of course—some plans
are just too grandiose or complex to pilot—but you'd be surprised how
many things you can test if you're creative and flexible. The beauty of
pilot projects is that you're usually not investing a ton of time or money
in them, which means you probably won't have as much opposition as
you would to a full-blown plan.

Innovation districts, anchor institutions, and governments can all
help conduct, embrace, and support pilot projects. At the BNMC, we
have a proven reputation as a testing ground for dozens of new technologies and innovations. That's one reason why the U.S. Department
of Transportation chose us to identify ways that underserved populations can travel to and from a campus without a personal automobile.
Once we work with our partners to show what works here—whether
that's accessible trip-planning applications, pedestrian safety technologies, or other innovations—we hope to help develop replicable, scalable solutions for other communities. Similarly, we're partnering with
Ellicottville Greens, an indoor hydroponic farming company that grows
lettuce, basil, and arugula inside refurbished shipping containers. One
of their shipping container gardens will be a demonstration site on our
campus, where we can grow food year-round for hospitals and a food
pantry while also providing educational programming for patients, staff,
visitors, and people throughout the community.

Prototypes are exciting because they help bring a vision to life, as we'll
talk about more in the next chapter. However, I encourage you to remain
focused on the equity component. Las Vegas, for example, is home

to hundreds of these tests, thanks in part to a streamlined, business-friendly approval process.[7] But they've also faced criticism for being too business-focused and not community-minded enough. Because pilot projects tend to be fast-tracked and limited in scope, you often don't get the full range of input and feedback from the community. As a result, you may inadvertently miss opportunities to maximize the equity-related impact.

Be Bold

Perhaps the one thing all visionaries have in common is that they aren't afraid of bold ideas.

In Buffalo, the African Heritage Food Co-Op has a slogan: "Because anything less than ownership is unacceptable." The Co-Op and its founder, Alexander J. Wright, have taken a stand. They're not just trying to eliminate food deserts. Their goal is real equity through food sovereignty, and their memorable slogan helps guide the way.

Whether it's full ownership of the food supply chain, ending homelessness, saving lives, or some other goal, if you're going to have a vision, make it stand out. Throughout our innovation district, we say that we are reimagining our city's future. Bold words inspire bold actions.

CHAPTER 9
Embrace the Activists

As we wrote in one of our first master plan updates, "What makes a campus a campus is its sense of place." When we first created the Buffalo Niagara Medical Campus (BNMC), we didn't have much money, but we wanted people to recognize that the campus was a special place. We couldn't really afford big signs or banners. So we got a few gallons of blue paint—the same color as our logo—and went out one day and painted all of the fire hydrants on the campus. As I recall, the fire commissioner wasn't very happy about us defacing city property. But, in our defense, we didn't break anything. People noticed. And it helped us build buzz for the new innovation district, so we could bring more people together for our equity-related initiatives.

If you want to get noticed, sometimes it's best to act first and ask for permission later—especially if you're faced with tight budgets, layers of bureaucracy, and entrenched standards. You don't need a lot of resources to make a difference. Often, all it takes is creativity, a willingness to think beyond traditional methods, and the ability to support those who do the same. That's what we'll be talking about in this chapter.

One Step at a Time

The other day, around lunchtime, I happened to see someone walking toward their car in the parking lot across from my office. On their way to their car, they noticed a small, eye-level sign that says, "It is a 4 minute walk to food trucks," with an arrow pointing up the street. They looked toward their car in the parking lot, back at the sign, then put their keys in their pocket and started walking toward the food trucks.

We put this sign up to encourage foot traffic in the innovation district.

The sign wasn't an official street sign, put up by the city. We printed it and hung it there ourselves, inspired by the Walk [Your City] movement. Walk [Your City] started one rainy night in Raleigh, when a group of people posted signs at three local intersections encouraging citizens to walk to nearby destinations. Since then, institutions and innovation districts from New York City to small towns in West Virginia have officially embraced these pedestrian-oriented wayfinding signs.

The signs are one of my favorite examples of "tactical urbanism," a phrase that describes an approach to improving cities "using short-term, low-cost, and scalable interventions and policies."[1] The phrase was created by Mike Lydon, who also wrote a book by the same name. In the book, Lydon interviewed one of the founders of the Walk [Your City] movement, who said he got the idea when people kept telling him places were "too far" to walk to.[2] The founders made a map of the places people were going and discovered that most of the destinations were actually just a few minutes by foot. What I love about this story is that the founders followed key principles of social design—listening to people and focusing on the problem—to discover that "the actual distance wasn't the problem, it was the *perception* of that distance."[3]

The Benefits of Tactical Urbanism

I can talk to people for hours about the benefits of a more walkable city. Or I can take them outside our office, point to the food truck sign, and take a four-minute walk together to get some incredible burritos.

Just like the pilot tests and prototypes we talked about in the last chapter, tactical urbanism makes something real. People can see it, touch it, walk around it, and react to it. They can see how it makes their lives better. Perhaps most importantly, it counters the emotional response—fear—that often accompanies something new or different.

With tactical urbanism, there isn't a long, drawn-out process. One day, you have the idea. The next day, it's right there, zip-tied to a light pole. And because there isn't as much formality, it's often a lot easier to involve key stakeholders to engage and inspire them.

Identify the best opportunities to use tactical urbanism in your work, being careful not to overuse these tactics. Remember, we just painted the fire hydrants—not the lamp poles and sidewalks, too. If something is ubiquitous, it just blends into the fabric of the city. And if you try to do too many unsanctioned activities, you're more likely to be forced to stop.

Think about the materials you're using and what people are already accustomed to. We didn't cover the hydrants with glitter or glue ribbons on them. We just used a different color of paint. If you can stick to standard materials, you may find fewer objections to your work.

Finally, make sure you're testing something that's feasible in the long term. If it's not, then what's the point? For example, it seems like a great idea to turn a parking lot into a community garden. But a garden will require significantly more upkeep than a parking lot, which means more time and money year after year after year. Who will do the work? Who will pay for it? If you can't answer those types of questions, you may want to reconsider your plans.

Process Matters

Often, in my opinion, activists are too focused on the results and don't pay enough attention to the process. Yes, the results are what ultimately matter. But how you plan to get there often determines whether you'll be successful in the long run.

If you're an activist (or supporting them), consider how you're going to communicate your plans with everyone, including other activists, government, law enforcement, the media, and your opponents. What are you doing, why are you doing it, and how will it help the community?

Unfortunately, authorities and those in power often have a knee-jerk response to activists and their work. Cities threaten to fine or arrest them, which is certainly justified if their actions are putting people at risk. (You can't just go around removing stop signs, for example.) Officials may also feel threatened by activists telling them how to do their jobs. But just because you have a college degree in urban planning doesn't mean you're always going to be right. And just because residents live in the neighborhood doesn't mean they know about accessibility, liability, and other issues that need to be addressed. As is often the case, the best approach is working together.

If you want to improve the chance that you'll succeed, think about what the decision makers really care about. Because even if they don't agree with your tactics, you're more likely to make progress if your results are aligned with their goals. Start by reading up on official city documents, including the city charter, meeting agendas, committee reports, and policy statements. Watch speeches from the mayor and legislators. Follow elected officials on social media and see what their priorities are. You may be able to justify your actions—and attract supporters—by showing how your work helps officials achieve their stated goals. Of course, you can apply this process to various levels of government, as well as within institutions and other organizations.

You're also more likely to get a win if you can save someone money. Can you save your city 1,000 hours of employee labor by supplying volunteers to clean up a park? If so, you're likely to get someone's attention. Look for ways to repurpose resources and reduce maintenance costs. Tactical urbanism—like pilots and prototypes—should be cost-effective. Remember, it's a test. If it works, then you can invest more to make it permanent. If you're spending a ton of time and money up front, you may want to rethink your approach. (That said, "temporary" and "permanent" are not the only states; there's a range, and projects can move along the scale from more temporary toward more permanent.)

Finally, don't discount public opinion. If it's a good idea, people will jump on board. And elected officials respond to public support. If you can prove that the community has your back, you're more likely to succeed.

Expectations versus Reality

"I think what people initially thought was that the Buffalo Niagara Medical Campus was going to be a silver bullet," said Stephanie Simeon, executive director of Heart of the City Neighborhoods, an organization that helps people find affordable housing. "People thought the medical campus would have the power to stop development in the neighborhood. But I think people attributed to them way more than what their mission is."

As Simeon points out, activists and those with an activist mindset sometimes misunderstand what an anchor institution or innovation district can do—and, perhaps more importantly, can't do. When these expectations don't align with the reality of what the organizations can accomplish, you end up with resentment and frustration all around.

Simeon is quick to note dozens of things that our innovation district could do, from advocating with the mayor's office for sidewalk repairs to offering a van that takes seniors to the grocery store. Some of these things are within our direct control (such as the grocery store van), and some aren't (replacing sidewalks). But even with the things we can do, we're still addressing only the symptom, not the underlying issues. After all, we can't single-handedly change the fact that the neighborhood is a food desert. That's why one of our most important tasks is to let activists know what to expect from us, so we can put our collective energy toward constructive partnerships.

Loopholes and Consequences

Activists look for loopholes. If you're looking for opportunities to make a difference, it may help to pay attention to what the regulations *don't* say instead of focusing on what they do. In 2005, three urban planners in San Francisco found an empty parking spot, fed the parking meter, and then filled the space with live grass, a park bench, and a potted tree, thus launching the global Park(ing) Day movement. After all, the parking regulations didn't say that you had to put a vehicle in a parking spot or that you couldn't put down grass and a bench. You're just paying for temporary use of the space.

Part of being an activist (and supporting activists) is understanding that there may be consequences for unsanctioned actions. One way to minimize these consequences is to know the rules. Read up on all relevant regulations. Print them out and have them with you. Look for ways to make your actions easily reversible—for example, by using chalk rather than paint. Most elected officials want to help the community, so if they're on your side, make it easy for them to support you by showing that you understand the rules, and you're making a well-informed, intentional decision.

Embrace Uncertainty

Activism is often about trying something new. There's going to be risk. As with almost any new endeavor, you're not going to know exactly what will happen as a result. That's okay.

As an activist, you also have to be patient. "Advocates don't like to have to wait," said Janice Henderson, who helped lead a project to restore Boston's Muddy River. The river, part of the city's famed Emerald Necklace park system designed by Frederick Law Olmsted, was being restored in a decades-long project supported by MASCO (the Medical Academic and Scientific Community Organization), where Henderson is a senior planner. "There were times when people were really frustrated and would try to push things along," said Henderson. "But working with an Olmstedian plan it can take a century to see the end result. You learn to become more patient watching trees grow and the plan come into form." Even when you're not waiting for Mother

Nature, solving complex problems takes time. We're not going to eliminate racial inequity in a month, a year, or probably even a decade, no
matter how urgent and pressing our work may be.

Where Activists Come From

Can I pay my rent? How long will I live? Am I happy?

Think back to the social design process and you'll see why it's critical
to understand not just what activists are fighting for—but why they're
so passionate. From lead-poisoned water in Flint, Michigan, to housing
displacement in San Francisco, these are issues that affect people on a
core basis. Whereas businesses and institutions may look at return on
investment or future growth plans when making decisions, for activists
these decisions are often seen in more stark terms: what is right, and
what is wrong. Don't underestimate activists, especially when it comes
to equity-related causes. It may take time (the Montgomery bus boycott
lasted more than a year), but activists are in it for the long haul.

Activists are often the ones doing a lot of the groundwork—canvas-
sing neighborhoods, gathering input from residents, and understanding
what people in the community truly need and want. You won't often
find better input than this.

When looking for activists, consider religious leaders. You may not
think of them as activists, but pastors and rabbis and imams and others
are already picking up where others leave off. "Because we are more in
tune and in touch with the people, it becomes our responsibility to take
the plight of the people to those who do not have the heart of the people," said Pastor William Gillison on the Talking Cities podcast.[4] Pastor
Gillison, who is part of the "Better Together" group of pastors that we
work with, founded a development corporation to help revitalize the
local neighborhood and was a lead voice in trying to change local school
board elections from May to November in order to increase turnout.

Dealing with Conflict

At some point—whether you're in an anchor institution, innovation district, government, or some other large institution—the activists will probably be fighting against you. When that happens, I usually try to engage with them, but if that's not working then just move on.

Some activists may (understandably) be hesitant to work with institutions or groups that represent authority. I remember my first meeting with one grassroots group, where the president of that group started off by saying that she's an activist, and she knows how to organize people and go after institutions. She gave me her list of what she wanted to accomplish for the community—and was very surprised when I said that those were my goals, too. Throughout the years, many activists have expected us to fight back. But there's no reason to fight if you're on the same page. In many cases, you'll agree on the problem and just need to work together on solutions.

It's important to understand exactly who the activists are representing, including who's funding them. Here in Buffalo, I've seen New York State assemblymember Crystal Peoples-Stokes stand up at community meetings and call out activists who aren't from the neighborhood but are just there to stir things up and get a grant for something that the people who live there don't actually want. You need elected officials like Peoples-Stokes who aren't afraid to represent the community and challenge activists who may have ulterior motives.

What Is Your Role?

I highly recommend embracing the activists. Anchor institutions and innovation districts can start by working closely with grassroots organizations, which often have more experience with these types of activist tactics. If there's someone out there who's already doing the work at the ground level, step aside and follow their lead. Don't let your ego get in the way. And don't mistake the size of an organization (or the credentials of its members) for its ability to get things done.

Organizations and institutions can support activists by sharing the resources they have, whether that's meeting space, equipment, or expertise. Here in Buffalo, our innovation district offers event space that's open to local organizations. We can also help cities save money. For example, in the historic Allentown neighborhood bordering the BNMC, the community association painted rainbow crosswalks to promote inclusivity for LGBTQ+ residents and businesses. More crosswalk art throughout the city—and on the BNMC—is planned for the future. To me, this is yet another sign of a growing trend: anchor institutions and innovation districts helping to fill roles that cash-strapped cities once undertook.

But if you're in a position of power, perhaps your most useful role is to support others. When we painted the fire hydrants, I knew they probably weren't going to fine me or make me face any serious consequences. After all, I was president of the innovation district, I worked closely with the mayor, I'm a White man, and I had connections to the top business leaders in town. (And yes, I recognize that all of these factors are related.) It's important to recognize that those in power—typically White men—often have greater freedom to support and engage in unsanctioned tactical urbanism. The tactical urbanism movement is sometimes criticized for its lack of diversity, but the reality is that people of color often face a different response from authorities if they're involved in unsanctioned activities. Those of us who have power and privilege can protect those who don't.

Even when race isn't a factor, formal organizations and institutions can also provide cover for unsanctioned groups. When activists added crosswalks and pylons to an intersection in Hamilton, Ontario, the actions earned a strong rebuke from city officials, which called them "illegal" and "vandalism." The next day, the Hamilton/Burlington Society of Architects sent a letter to the city, siding with the activists who "have taken it upon themselves to try to make the city a better place," referencing the city's own master plans, and offering to meet with city officials to find the best ways to improve the city.[5] Think about ways that you can use your position to publicly support activists.

Similarly, consider ways you can eliminate the obstacles that are blocking activists. One way to do this is to recognize and call out inequity when you see it. For example, are Black-owned firms treated equitably in every step of the procurement process? Andrew Colas, president of a Black-owned construction company, recalled interviewing for a contract to renovate the Oregon Convention Center and being asked whether his firm would have bonding capacity for such a large project. But before he could reply, someone on the selection committee intervened. "'Don't answer that question, it wasn't asked of any of the other participants.'"[6]

Finally, look for ways to be proactive. Activists are out there fighting against inequitable conditions. If you can remove those conditions—or prevent them from being put in place to start with—you can have a significant impact. What dress codes are you enforcing? How do your community's zoning regulations define a family? What is the priority for cars versus pedestrians in your city? Addressing equity-related issues before they cause more harm may not be as exhilarating as marching in a protest but can often be just as effective.

CHAPTER 10
Build Better Bridges

"People don't invite young Black people like me to meet with them regularly."

That's what one of the people I work with told me the other day. And he was right. So I started asking people from throughout the community—especially those who weren't typically invited to the table—to meet and talk.

One of the first guys I met is a designer who runs events that attract up to 2,500 young Black adults. He said he was trying to get a sponsorship from a well-known locally based company, but they weren't returning his calls. Meanwhile, I knew that the CEO of the company wanted to partner with more Black trendsetters but didn't know where to start. Both of them wanted to connect, but neither of them had a direct line to the other. So I made an introduction. I built a bridge. Similarly, I met a young Black man who was planning a music and arts festival, and I was able to connect him with multiple CEOs throughout the community.

Bridges bring us together. They help us overcome obstacles and go new places. We need more bridges—and better bridges—to succeed as a community and ensure that everyone has the opportunities they need to advance.

Integrated Networks

Although I like making introductions and having these "At the Table" meetings (I borrowed the name from events hosted by The Chicago Community Trust), it's not a scalable approach. I don't always want to be the guy in the middle. I want to create integrated networks, which connect the networks that are already out there. Once people are connected, they can start making more connections within that network, then their connections can make connections, and so on.

I've certainly benefited many times from these types of connections. For example, when there was a dispute involving our organization and a local union, a pastor I know arranged a meeting between me and the head of the union, which helped us get off to a good start. In every city, there are people who span multiple communities, who can help you build bridges from one group to another. Look for these people and recognize their potential to accelerate the creation of integrated networks.

Integrating networks takes time. It takes trust. It takes humility to recognize that even if you're well connected in the traditional sense, you still don't have access to many (or even most) of the networks within your community. And it takes generosity and foresight to share your network with others, even when there's nothing in it for you.

And yes, I realize that there's still a power dynamic here. As CEO of the innovation district, I'm the one inviting people to my table. I'm the one with access to elected officials and other CEOs and capital. But that's exactly what needs to change. People shouldn't have to go through me. We need fewer gatekeepers and more open doors.

EforAll

One way we're integrating networks is through a program called Entrepreneurship for All (EforAll) and a companion program called Entrepreneurs Forever (eforever). EforAll is a national movement that has helped create more than five hundred startups in cities like Buffalo that don't necessarily have huge innovation hubs. In each city, EforAll typically works with thirty mainly minority-owned, women-owned, and immigrant-owned growing businesses each year, providing mentors and other resources to help spur new connections.

I think we've been good at *facilitating* these types of bridges in the past, but we haven't always done the best job of *nurturing* them. There are entrepreneurs all over Buffalo who still don't feel welcome in the flourishing startup ecosystem here—especially people of color and women, who often face discrimination and other obstacles when building a business. That's what EforAll is designed to change. We're building a robust, open innovation community, with access to connections, financial opportunities, business support services, and much more. People can join as members, whether they're leasing space in one of our buildings or not. By purposefully integrating networks—and caring for those connections on a long-term basis—we can help communities grow from within. As one of only eleven EforAll sites in the country as I write this, we're excited to be at the forefront of advancing equity and inclusion in Buffalo's innovation ecosystem. (We're also grateful to senator Charles Schumer and his staff, who introduced us to EforAll through his efforts to ensure that underrepresented communities were fairly included in economic recovery and stimulus programs.)

Connecting Institutions and Communities

Bridges—both literal and symbolic—can bring people together in new and unexpected ways. But a bridge doesn't always have to be a bridge.

Take a stroll through Buffalo's Allentown neighborhood, listed on the National Register of Historic Places, and you'll see houses adorned with arched windows, stone carvings, and intricate wood scrolls. Formerly home to F. Scott Fitzgerald and Frederick Law Olmsted, Allentown continues to attract some of the city's most prominent citizens.

Allentown borders the Buffalo Niagara Medical Campus (BNMC), which means that what happens in Allentown affects the campus and vice versa. So when the University at Buffalo wanted to build a new six-story medical school on the campus directly adjacent to Allentown, we went to the community for input. They told us that they wanted to keep the campus open to the community, so it would be easy for people on campus to take a short walk to Allentown's popular restaurants and boutique shops. The dean of the school, Michael Cain, listened carefully to their concerns and asked the architects and designers to find a solution. As a result, the medical school features a spacious pedestrian passageway through the heart of the building, connecting Allentown with the medical campus.

I joke that in this case a bridge is a hole, but it's true; a bridge is anything that brings people together.

Why not just put restaurants and retail on the ground floor of our buildings, as many innovation districts have done, instead of sending them off campus? When we first created the campus, there were already dozens of successful shops, cafes, and other establishments in the surrounding neighborhoods, and we wanted to help them grow—not take away their loyal customers. It was all part of our master plan. (That said, even without retail and restaurants in the pedestrian passageway, perhaps there's an opportunity to make it more inviting by adding tables, chairs, benches, and other features that could transform a functional walkway into a welcoming destination.)

Bridges don't build themselves. If you want people to interact, you need to be intentional about the systems, processes, and infrastructure you design.[1] In Buffalo, Ellicott Park runs through the spine of the innovation district, connecting institutions and neighborhoods alike. The linear park—36 feet wide and six blocks long—features islands, plazas, and custom "inward" and "outward" benches from the design firm (nARCHITECTS) that encourage interactions and bring people together.

Relationships Build Bridges

At one point, I was negotiating on behalf of one of our anchor institutions that needed to buy six homes in order to have the land for a new facility. I went to these homes and sat in the living rooms with the homeowners. I walked the neighborhood with them, trying to help them find new places to live. Most of them accepted an offer fairly quickly. But one family had been there for more than fifty years and simply didn't want to move at any price. I met with them countless times. We had offered them enough to buy multiple new homes in the neighborhood, all of their moving expenses, taxes for a decade, and even free healthcare for life. They still said no.

I honestly didn't know what else I could do. So I called them the next day and said, "Can you do me a favor? Can you do this transaction for me?"

They said okay.

At some point, it wasn't about the money. It was about the relationship that we built by seeing each other as people—not as obstacles or part of a financial transaction. And yes, in the end, we got what we wanted. I'll never know exactly why they said yes when they did, but I'd like to think it was because I was just a human being trying to do the right thing for another person. If you ever find yourself wondering what to do, start by behaving like a neighbor, not an institution. "Just think about what you want for your grandma," says Stephanie Simeon, executive director of Heart of the City Neighborhoods, "and act like a human being."

Bridges at Work

Nick Hopkins's epiphany came in a hotel ballroom in Wyoming.

Neurosurgeon L. Nelson "Nick" Hopkins had organized a conference with some of the top cardiologists, vascular surgeons, and radiologists in the world, so they could learn from each other's mistakes. But he realized that one of their biggest mistakes was seeing each other only once or twice a year. Even though they all worked on patients' arteries and veins, they rarely talked to each other, even when they were colleagues in the same building.

To treat vascular disease—the number-one cause of death worldwide—Hopkins envisioned a center that would bring together all of these disciplines, along with clinicians and scientists, under one roof. Hopkins began brainstorming with architect Mehrdad Yazdani, who realized they needed a building that would force collisions between people, which is exactly what he and design lead Craig Booth envisioned. The resulting ten-story building is designed like a club sandwich, says Hopkins, with scientists on the top, clinicians on the bottom, and an innovation center in the middle where they share and apply their life-saving learnings. Throughout the building, cafes and open staircases bring people together in even more ways. Having multiple groups in one building—something you'll often find in innovation districts—is a natural way to build bridges. Building one facility with co-located institutions also saved approximately $15 million, which makes it an even more appealing model.

Regardless of your physical facilities, think about what bridges you have to communicate with co-workers, peers, and leaders. Are these one-way channels, or is there flow back and forth? Who *don't* you have a bridge to—and why not? In my experience, many large institutions are better at internal communications than people give them credit for, especially given that they can easily have thousands of people working together. But there's always room for improvement.

Think about how you and your colleagues can build bridges that span social divides. I'm inspired by people like Megan Smith, former chief technology officer of the United States and a proud Buffalo native. As founder and CEO of shift7, Smith leads a team that leverages collaborations to achieve greater impact, including matching diverse coders and engineers with talent-hungry companies and helping researchers show the entertainment industry how to mitigate gender bias in film.

Practical, Symbolic, or Both?

Think about whether your bridge needs to fill a practical need, a symbolic purpose, or both. In the early days of the BNMC, some of our largest funders were concerned about the existing culture of noncooperation between institutions. So when two institutions were planning new buildings across the street from each other, our funders insisted that we have a skybridge connecting the facilities. The bridge wasn't going to be cheap. There were a lot of design problems, and it became fairly controversial for many reasons. But we built it, and today it serves as a well-traveled conduit and a gateway to the campus and tells people that this is where we work together.

Symbols matter. In 2020, we saw protesters and governments alike tear down Confederate monuments and proudly paint "Black Lives Matter" on city streets. Statues and signs are bridges, both to a community's past and to its core values today. They can signal that people are welcome or that they should stay out. What do your symbols say?

The Role of Anchor Institutions and Innovation Districts

As an anchor institution or innovation district, there are many things you can do to build bridges. But before you start, look for the people who are already doing the work and think about ways you can support them. In Buffalo, Rev. Darius Pridgen has made his church a connection point for the community to get vital services. He opened a restaurant inside the church to provide job training, transformed a school bus into a mobile clothing pantry, and offers "freedom funerals" for homicide victims—providing the funeral and wake at no charge for families if they allow the church to have social service agencies available to talk with residents.

So what can anchor institutions and innovation districts do? Like many of our peers, we typically have filled calendars with events open to the public, including Beakers and Beer networking events and an annual Student Open House for children to tour research and educational facilities. These serve as a bridge within organizations that make up the innovation district, as well as to the community. Of course, you should also be thinking about how you can bring your anchor institution or innovation district into the community. Meeting people where they are with pop-up events, community shuttles, and other initiatives can help people learn about an organization without leaving home. We can't force people to engage with us, but we should certainly make it easier for them to do so. (Taking that a step further, some organizations are "de-anchoring" their institutions by completely moving them outside traditional innovation districts or by creating additional locations. In Medellín, Colombia, city leaders plan to open nearly two dozen satellite innovation centers throughout the city. Although de-anchoring has the potential to build more bridges, it's paramount that you understand the diversity and uniqueness of each neighborhood in order to be effective.)

Procurement programs are another common bridge. Here in Buffalo, Kaleida Health has an award-winning purchasing program, thanks to their efforts to ensure diversity and inclusion among their suppliers. An innovation district–wide Farm-to-Hospital program helps connect local farmers with healthcare institutions (and their hungry patients, visitors, and staff). In Cleveland, the University Circle innovation district supports the Evergreen Cooperative Initiative, which helps create and strengthen minority-owned businesses in nearby low-income neighborhoods. "The idea is that proximity matters, and that neighborhood residents should be owning and profiting from that work," said Chris Ronayne, president of University Circle. "The bedsheets are turned over every night at the hospital, so why go to a third exurb suburb to have the sheets cleaned?" noted Ronayne. Today, the Evergreen initiative includes a commercial laundry, an energy solutions group, and a greenhouse where employees learn to grow high-quality organic vegetables.

Digging into your supply chain may yield some surprises, too. We found that vendors, distributors, and institutions didn't always know exactly where their food purchases were coming from. In one case, more than half of the purchases had unidentifiable sources—a discovery that helped us convince local hospitals to build stronger connections to their food sources.

Long-term, permanent jobs are perhaps the most important piece of the puzzle when it comes to advancing equity in a community. A paycheck often leads to better housing, access to healthcare, and countless other quality-of-life improvements. Yet many people are excluded from jobs in anchor institutions and innovation districts because they don't have a four-year (bachelor's) degree, even though it isn't necessarily needed to do many of the jobs.

"If I examined the Buffalo Niagara Medical Campus, I would probably find that 30 percent or more of those jobs really don't require a four-year degree," said Tom Osha, chairman of the board of The Global Institute on Innovation Districts. "They may be coded for a four-year degree, but they can likely be reclassified to match what an associate's degree delivers and broaden the number of people who can participate in these jobs."

We should all be thinking about how we can build a more accessible bridge between the community and these jobs. For example, more cities are starting to develop partnerships between innovation districts, universities, and community colleges, giving students clearer paths from high school to a four-year university, or from community college straight into a high-tech job.

"There are a lot of people who cannot wait four years to have an undergraduate degree because they need to get income as soon as possible," said Carlos Jaramillo, the science, technology, and innovation solutions developer at Ruta N innovation district in Medellín, Colombia. "I remember one guy who used to deliver food in the city. He decided to learn how to program through a two-year apprentice program, got an internship, and he's now one of the top automation test programmers for a multinational company."

And when you're thinking about jobs, consider those who are often overlooked. Some hospitals and other anchor institutions are reviewing their policies for hiring ex-offenders, given the inequalities in incarceration rates for Black and Brown people and the related systemic racial inequities that can lead to imprisonment.

Schools as a Bridge

In many cities, anchor institutions and innovation districts work closely with K–12 schools and early childhood education centers, in part because of schools' ability to be a natural bridge between the institutions and the community, as well as their unique role in creating more equitable communities. Here in Buffalo, the innovation district has helped provide computers for students and worked with parent groups and others to improve the schools. That said, getting involved with schools and childcare centers is often a tough sell to anchor institutions and innovation districts, in part because (as with many equity-related initiatives) there's not a direct, immediate benefit. The results can easily take decades to see, which is something to consider when you're building bridges. How long are you willing to wait for the results?

Speaking of schools, as we saw during the COVID pandemic, digital bridges are increasingly important in terms of equity. Having a computer, tablet, or smartphone—as well as access to a stable, high-speed internet connection—is all but essential for students, workers, and anyone wanting to connect with the world. As the pandemic highlighted this digital divide, many school districts, startups, and other organizations nationwide built trust with their communities (and helped students and working parents alike) by equipping school buses and trailers with Wi-Fi and sending them out to areas with unreliable internet service. Wi-Fi is a bridge.

How You Can Help

In times of crisis, anchor institutions can also serve as a bridge to vital resources and information, whether it's treatment for patients with COVID-19 at hospitals, insight into historical racism and the rise of the Black Lives Matter movement from museums, or climate change research from universities.

How can you be a bridge between the community and other institutions? For example, research has shown that new, Black-owned businesses have one third as much capital than White-owned businesses, partly because Black entrepreneurs fear their loan applications will be rejected.[2] But what if we can take away this fear by bridging the gap between Black entrepreneurs and lending institutions?

Organizations and communities alike can also leverage their partners to help them with bridge building. We've seen this with construction contracts from government agencies, requiring developers to pay a certain wage, employ a specified percentage of people from underserved communities, or include other opportunities and benefits for neighbor-ing areas. Consider what you can encourage (or require) your partners to do and how you can hold them to a higher standard when it comes to equity.

Build Carefully

The Indianapolis Cultural Trail: A Legacy of Gene and Marilyn Glick zigs and zags through the heart of the city, an 8-mile collection of urban trails connecting half a dozen downtown cultural districts.

By many measures, the Cultural Trail is an unprecedented success, used by more than a million people each year, from shift workers biking to jobs, to seniors out for a leisurely stroll, to museum-hopping tourists (although there's certainly a distinction between those who must walk or bike and those who choose to). The trail has helped take countless cars off the streets and serves as a top draw for convention planners.[3]

"The Cultural Trail really brings you within a block of every major cultural, arts, sporting, heritage, historical destination that you would want to go to in downtown Indianapolis," explains Kären Haley, exec-utive director of Indianapolis Cultural Trail Inc., a nonprofit organi-zation. It has also helped many small businesses, says Haley, recalling a family-owned sandwich restaurant that has doubled in size since the trail opened. "You can just say you're on the Cultural Trail and people will find you."

In terms of improving equity, the Cultural Trail—which is available twenty-four hours a day—is free to use, improves accessibility (yes, they clear the snow in the winter), offers a bike share and adaptive bike pro-gram, helps extend the public transportation system, and serves as a lin-ear park. The trail has undoubtedly brought people together. But it has also driven some away through gentrification and displacement. Studies have shown that the assessed property values have increased by a total of $1 billion along the trail. In some cases, a rapid increase in the cost of housing meant some residents couldn't afford to live there anymore.[4]

Although much of the development along the Cultural Trail occurred in areas filled with abandoned buildings and parking lots, noted Haley, she and her team are keeping affordable housing at the forefront. They're thinking about how to minimize displacement for educational institutions and small businesses on what Haley calls the Cultural Trail's "beachfront property." And they're reaching out to potential community partners who have experience in affordable housing, to proactively purchase property along transit routes and preserve affordable housing.

Bridges must be built thoughtfully and intentionally in order to achieve the desired results. It's important to think about unintended consequences and potential failures.

I'm not picking on Indianapolis here. I could choose any city in the country—including Buffalo—and point out a dozen "bridges" that had unintended side effects. As always, think through your decisions with an equity lens, the sooner the better. Talk with the people who may be affected by the bridge. After all, you want your bridge to connect people, not force them further apart.

A Few More Words of Caution

If you're building a bridge, think about the timing—in terms of both how long it will take to build and when you should be building it. Some bridges can be built in a minute with just a handshake and an introduction. Others take decades.

When you build a bridge too soon, it can feel forced. If people aren't ready to work together, you can't make them. There's almost always a bit of tension when you first start, so if you're getting pushback, find out if it's because people really aren't ready for the bridge or if it's just the friction you'll find in nearly any new venture.

What happens more often, in my experience, is that you build a bridge too late and end up with missed opportunities. If I had started my "At the Table" meetings at my house ten years ago, I could have helped make hundreds of additional connections by now, each of which could have spawned countless others. Don't wait.

Bridges are also difficult to unbuild. Once I've had someone over to my house, I'm not likely to ignore them when they email or call me. Indianapolis isn't going to tear down their Cultural Trail. It's not impossible, of course—but bridges tend to last a while.

Building and Rebuilding

A few blocks from my office is the new John R. Oishei Children's Hospital, the only freestanding children's hospital in New York State. In the years leading up to the opening, the plans for the hospital were shaped by numerous New York State governors, each with a different vision for the facility.

After every election, anchor institutions and innovation districts need to establish relationships with elected officials. That's part of the job. (At least these transitions occur on a fairly regular, public schedule, unlike with community leaders, hospital CEOs, university presidents, and others, who may leave at any time, often unexpectedly.)

As you build bridges, consider how you can fortify them to survive and thrive through transitions. A bridge between two CEOs isn't nearly as strong as a bridge that also includes multiple senior and junior staff on both sides.

Not Everyone Wants a Bridge

When swimming pools became desegregated, cities that kept their pools open saw White attendance fall up to 95 percent.[5] Here in Western New

York, the largest mall in the region welcomed buses from the suburbs but not from the city—until Cynthia Wiggins, a Black teenager from Buffalo, was killed after taking the bus and trying to cross a seven-lane street to get to the mall.[6] Buses from Wiggins's city neighborhood were allowed at the mall after the NAACP, Urban League, and Buffalo Teachers Federation threatened to boycott the mall. It takes more work to build a bridge when the people in power don't want it to exist.

If you're building bridges, you'll probably run into opposition, veiled or not, from people who don't want to be connected to others. But what exactly are they opposed to? It's probably not the bridge itself but rather what's on the other side. Understand what's fueling the opposition, whether it's a desire to keep the status quo, fear of the unknown, or—as we've seen time and time again—outright racism, intolerance, and discrimination.

Finally, just as we talked about the differences between opportunity and access, there is a notable difference between building a bridge and putting it to use for the good of the community. Simply bringing high-speed internet service to a low-income neighborhood, for example, doesn't close the income inequality gap. The bridge is just the connection, the starting point, a way for someone to get from one point to another. There's almost always more work to be done.

CHAPTER 11
Know When to Take the Back Seat

Four-year-old Katherine Gioia wasn't feeling well. Her parents thought it could be pneumonia, but a chest X-ray revealed their worst nightmare: a rare form of cancer.

Katherine asked her mom to tell the doctors she didn't have time to be sick. But she didn't have a choice. They went to Roswell Park Comprehensive Cancer Center in Buffalo, where they fought day after exhausting day through grueling treatments. But in the end, there was nothing anyone could do to stop the cancer from taking young Katherine's life.

When Katherine died, her family knew their work wasn't done. What they didn't know was that Katherine's death would lead to the birth of the Buffalo Niagara Medical Campus (BNMC) and inspire a movement that would raise nearly half a billion dollars.

In Katherine's memory, her mom, her aunt, and a friend started the Roswell Park Alliance Foundation to support the cancer center. The timing was critical, because Roswell Park's funding from New York State was at risk of being cut. But Anne Gioia, Donna Gioia, and Pam Jacobs—the three "Roswell Women," as they came to be known—were fighting for Katherine's legacy and for an entire community of loved ones lost.[1]

Thanks in large part to the women's tireless efforts, New York State approved the funding that would transform and modernize Roswell Park, including a new state-of-the-art patient center—a ten-story-tall sign of progress and hope. Elected officials took notice, developers took an interest, and just a few years later we officially established the BNMC, with Roswell Park as one of the lead institutions. The Roswell Park Alliance Foundation has continued its efforts and has now raised more than $450 million (and counting) to support research, education, and patient care.

Like most people in our community, I have friends who owe their lives to the care they received at Roswell Park. I appreciate the work that Roswell does to promote equity, including raising awareness of breast and cervical cancer among Black women, providing cancer screening for Latinas, and reducing the impact of cancer on Indigenous people and others who are disproportionately affected. The organization isn't without its critics, in part because of their ongoing growth adjacent to the Fruit Belt residential neighborhood. But their positive impact throughout our community is undeniable, and we can trace a lot of it back to the efforts inspired by Katherine Gioia. (It's also important to note that Roswell Park is led by Candace Johnson, the only female leader of the "big three" anchor institutions on the medical campus and a highly respected member of our board of directors.)

There are many ways in which anchor institutions and innovation districts can lead the way toward more equitable communities. But sometimes the most powerful change agents are people in the community. They're the ones who often have the most to gain—or, like Katherine's family, have already suffered incalculable loss and want to help others avoid that unbearable pain.

When the Community Leads

In any city, CEOs come and go. Elected officials are voted in and out. But the community is always there.

"What would cities look like if the people who lived in them, who made them function, controlled their fate?" asked P. E. Moskowitz in *How to Kill a City*.[2] This line of thinking is the natural extension of the social design process. Are we simply getting input from the community and inviting them to the table? Or do they actually have the power to enact change in their own communities?

At the BNMC, we've taken the back seat on a number of projects and continue to do so. These decisions are based partly on available resources; the staff of our innovation district and anchor institutions simply don't have the time to take a leadership role on every important project. But we also recognize that we don't always belong up front, nor is it always most effective for us to be there.

"Anchor institutions can only do so much," notes Marla Guarino, the Farm to Institution program coordinator at the BNMC. "You have to have those community partnerships to focus on equity in its entirety." When everyone has a sense of ownership, we are stronger, together.

When you think about taking a back seat, remember that you're not "letting" the community lead. They don't need your permission. It's their community just as much as it's yours.

Sparking Change

"The children on Mulberry and Maple, they use that park every day," said Annette Lott, talking about a popular pocket park where neighborhood kids come to jump and slide on the playground, climb the rock wall, or just enjoy a moment of shade beneath the towering trees.[3]

Lott is president of Fruit Belt United, the community organization that owns the park. Fruit Belt United partnered with The Foundry (a local community space) and the Fruit Belt Community Land Trust on a "Summer Spruce Up" project, which included a neighborhood cleanup, a workshop to teach people how to build raised planting beds, and installation of the raised beds at the playground.

The work was funded by BNMC Spark, a microgrant program offered through the BNMC. Through Spark grants we've funded dozens of community-led projects, including a sensory garden for people who are blind or visually impaired, free photography classes for children, and a mural planned by children and adults with intellectual and developmental disabilities.

The best part about Spark grants is that they help bring the community's vision to life. People come to us and tell us what they think is helpful and will make a difference. They're the ones coming up with the ideas to make Buffalo a better place. We simply review the applications and fund the best projects, ideally those that promote collaboration, have strong community support, and include plans for engaging the neighborhood to advance a more inclusive, vibrant city.

Amplify Others

With every project, it helps to have someone taking responsibility for moving things forward. But the leader doesn't always have to be the largest, wealthiest, or most well-connected organization.

Part of taking the back seat is recognizing which messages and movements would be more powerful—and more sustainable—coming from the community. These are the voices that are not only more authentic, they're also typically more trusted. Although they may not always have the reach that a large institution does—or the influence within political and corporate circles—anchor institutions and innovation districts can help them be heard. "We want to be an amplifier of the collective voice," explained Kyria Stephens, the BNMC director of inclusion and community initiatives. "It's not just about our message."

How do you amplify these voices? First you have to find them. Start with the people who represent the community. These are your influencers: the clergy, people who run community centers, business owners, block club leaders, and other well-respected residents. You'll find them in churches and corner stores, barber shops and restaurants, and anywhere that people gather and meet. Go there and listen to the people who are already doing the work. Before you start adding new ideas to the mix, think about ways you can help them with the projects that are already in play.

Be intentional about seeking out other networks. Think about equity from a broad perspective, and seek out voices from refugees, members of the LGBTQIA+ community, seniors, people with disabilities, and other groups that may currently be underserved and underrepresented.

Celebrate the community leaders who are working to create more equitable communities. In our podcast, *Talking Cities*, I've been fortunate enough to talk with dozens of these change makers, including the director of a library system that lends out more than four million items each year, the executive director of FoodShare Toronto, and an assemblywoman who has helped fight for minority- and women-owned business enterprise contracts. If you have a platform (even if it's just a social media account), think about how you can use it to elevate others.

Remember what we talked about in chapter 3: Check your ego at the door. It's not about you. If someone else can do the job better, let them. Focus on the results. As Sam Fiorello from the Cortex innovation district put it, "Cortex is a bright, shiny star—but it's a star in a constellation of others. Sometimes we're going to be the lead partner, and sometimes we're the supporting partner, and that's OK."

Go out of your way to give others the credit they deserve. It's not about who gets the headline today; it's about making the community stronger for tomorrow. Sure, there are times that you will want your anchor institution or innovation district to be visibly at the forefront. There's certainly a time for that. Just not every time.

Be a Convener

For more than seventy years, Boston's Muddy River—part of the city's Emerald Necklace park system designed by Frederick Law Olmsted— remained invisible after being channeled underground, partly buried below a Sears parking lot. But with the water flowing through under-sized 6-foot culverts, there were serious flooding problems, including one occurrence that shut down the Massachusetts Bay Transportation Authority Green Line for a week and caused nearly $70 million in dam-age to public infrastructure.

So local advocacy groups, government, and others started talking about ways to restore the river to its original grandeur while mitigat-ing the future flood risk. Traffic, safety, and flooding (linked to climate change and global warming) were the primary considerations, but the project would also improve pedestrian access to the subway and create a more resilient public transportation system, both of which were import-ant in terms of advancing equity.

The restoration was led by the U.S. Army Corps of Engineers and involved numerous groups, including the Emerald Necklace Conser-vancy, Brookline Preservation Commission, Boston Parks and Recre-ation Department, and Massachusetts Department of Conservation and Recreation, among others. But it was Boston's MASCO (Medical Aca-demic and Scientific Community Organization) innovation district that helped bring everyone together. MASCO's offices were in a convenient location and featured a conference room where representatives could meet and hash out their differences. MASCO officials were interested in the project because it affected their member institutions, especially in terms of traffic flow (they had to ensure that ambulances and essential workers could still get to local hospitals quickly). But most importantly, MASCO had a well-earned reputation as a convener. "That's what we do," said Tom Yardley, a vice president at MASCO.

When anchor institutions and innovation districts have earned trust in the community, they can accelerate progress simply by bringing everyone else together, even if they don't take the lead themselves. In fact, I argue that it's our *responsibility* as institutions to convene key stakeholders, address elected officials and others in power, and advocate for more equitable societies. Who can you bring together for a common cause?

You don't even have to be the convener to be helpful. You can support activists behind the scenes. You can lend your resources, whether it's office space or construction equipment or anything else. You can make introductions. Share the knowledge and insight that your co-workers have. Make a phone call to an elected official to vouch for a community-led project. None of these actions requires you to take the lead, but they can all be extraordinarily helpful in moving things forward.

The Importance of Volunteers

Especially in the early days of the BNMC, we were extremely fortunate to have the support and services of many community volunteers. These volunteers don't seek the spotlight. They aren't there for personal gain or to make headlines. They're just there to stay in the background and make a difference, which is what makes them so valuable.

A paycheck tends to pull most people in a certain direction, but volunteers pull for the community. They take the back seat. For the most part, we've been fortunate to have people who "wanted to do the right thing here and wanted to do it well," as former Buffalo mayor Tony Masiello noted. People like Tom Beecher, Bill Joyce, Tony Martino, Jim Biltekoff, David Zebro, and Ted Walsh were the selfless leaders who put

Buffalo first. I like to call them my "mentors without a motive," and I firmly believe that the BNMC would not exist without them.

That said, there's something else the volunteers I mentioned all have in common: They're all White men who were prominent business leaders and had the time and financial freedom to volunteer.

When you're soliciting volunteers, you need to recognize that not everyone can afford to volunteer. Those who can have a level of financial security that may make them less attuned to the needs of low-income residents. Not everyone is asked to volunteer, often because they're outside the traditional business-centric power circles. If your volunteers are predominantly White, as ours were, they'll never have firsthand perspective on the obstacles that Black and Brown people face. If they're mostly men, they won't experience inequities from a woman's point of view. If they're all heterosexual, they won't be as aware of LGBTQIA+ concerns. Our volunteers were representing the community, but they weren't representative *of* the community. Although I'm eternally grateful for the support our volunteers offered, we made a mistake by not doing more to find, recruit, and support a broader range of volunteers.

Stepping Back in Your Organization

When Tony Martino joined the board of directors in the early days of the BNMC, he had just retired as a partner at one of the region's most prestigious accounting firms. Everyone knew who he was. Meanwhile, I was barely out of my twenties. We went to meetings together, and people would expect Martino to get up and lead our presentation. Instead, I would stand up at the front of the room and begin talking. If anyone asked—and they did—Martino would just say, "I'm Matt's gray hair." He was there for backup, but it was my show. For me, it was a powerful lesson that people need to know when to take a back seat.

Today, even as head of the innovation district, I'm often the one taking the back seat. Just the other day, Kyria Stephens (who leads our community initiatives) and I were on a call with the head of a local professional organization. Right from the start, the person we were talking to was critical of our work, based mostly on what they had heard and read about us in the newspapers. So Stephens took over the call. He knows better than I do exactly what's happening in the neighborhoods, so he was able to speak in much more detail about the things we're doing to strengthen the community—and open up about the things we haven't addressed yet. Stephens has quickly become one of my mentors because, like other people on our team, he knows more than I do about many equity-related topics. Leaders need to recognize that they can be mentored, too.

That's the benefit of having a diverse team. Not just diverse in terms of race and gender and age and other factors but diverse in terms of the skills, knowledge, and perspective that each person offers. Thinking back to my days playing basketball, you need someone who can shoot three pointers, but you also need someone who can make the short jump shots. You're always going to need a team.

Stephens could put the other person's mind at ease in a way that I couldn't. He was the more trusted voice. He has expertise and experience that I do not. And he jumped in and took over the call because he knows that I trust him and that he's empowered to speak for the innovation district. If you're not comfortable taking the back seat within your organization, why not? And what does that say about you—and the people you work with? Taking the back seat isn't always easy. But it's often the best way to get where you want to go.

CHAPTER 12

Plan, but Be Flexible
(and Open to Serendipity)

"Oh sh#t."

It was mid-March of 2020, and everything—everything—was shutting down because of the COVID-19 pandemic. Schools sent students, teachers, and staff home for what was supposed to be a two-week break. Hospitals canceled elective surgeries. Restaurants switched to takeout-only. I started wearing a mask and carrying hand sanitizer everywhere and figuring out what comes next.

Fortunately, our innovation district has a master plan: a 272-page document that guides nearly everything we do. It outlines our goals, our vision, and our commitment to the community. I knew we weren't going to change our strategy and long-term focus, but everything else was on the table.

First of all, we cut our expenses quickly and drastically. (Like many innovation districts, most of our revenue comes from rent and parking fees, both of which took an immediate nosedive.) We furloughed staff, which wasn't an easy choice. These are friends, not just colleagues. But we made tough decisions and moved on, knowing there were more tough decisions still to be made. Fortunately, we had a strong yet flexible

CFO in Patrick Kilcullen; without him, it's doubtful our organization would have survived.

Advancing equity was already a core part of our mission, so we knew we would keep helping the community. We partnered with local organizations to increase food system resiliency. Our chief innovation officer, Sam Marrazzo, reached out to Mission: Ignite and Say Yes Buffalo to get home computers for dozens of students in the Buffalo Public School District, now learning from home. We supported our member institutions as they hosted vaccination centers, researched new treatments, and took care of their essential workers.

We had a solid plan. But plans and priorities change over time—sometimes overnight. When they do, you need to be ready. In this chapter, we'll discuss how a thoughtful, well-researched strategic plan will lay the groundwork for equity-focused efforts and provide the flexibility necessary to navigate nearly any challenge.

Have a Plan

I can't overemphasize how important it is to have a plan. A plan crystallizes your strategy and maps out your next steps. It's an opportunity to translate your values into actionable items. It makes you put things in writing, so everyone agrees on what you're doing and where you're going. The mere existence of a detailed plan can help build credibility with skeptics, because it shows that you've done the work. (My advice: Keep a hard copy handy to make an impression; our master plan is a 3-pound stack of paper that makes a satisfying "thunk" when you drop it on a conference room table.)

When you first start on your plan, recognize that governments, institutions, and community groups may all have vastly different expectations for the planning process. This can be a challenge when you have representatives from universities, hospitals, and city hall sitting at the table with staff from small nonprofit organizations and volunteers from local neighborhood associations. Some people will be comfortable with a planning process that takes months or even years to complete, and others will quickly become frustrated when things don't move at a faster pace. Be transparent and set the expectations (and a timeline) up front.

Start Small and Think Big

I look at my smartphone, and it's basically a big black rectangle with a screen on one side—almost exactly like the first one I bought a decade ago. The basic functionality really hasn't changed over the years, but each new model is just a little bit better.

If you spend too much time looking for ways to make massive, wholesale change, you're going to waste many, many hours. Instead, focus on the countless opportunities to make incremental adjustments that add up (and up and up) to significant improvements over the years. Small steps compounded over time can be surprisingly effective. And you may be surprised how quickly you get encouragement—or pushback—from the community, leading you in new directions.

You don't need to have a master plan your first day, first month, or even first year. Especially in the beginning, think about how you can use prototypes and incremental change to experiment with new ideas. Take the time to figure out who you are—and how you're going to work together—before you try to put it in writing. Understand whether you're planning for organic or intentional growth. Consider the opportunity costs; whatever you choose to do, you're essentially choosing *not* to do something else. Then write the things you're *not* going to do. It feels odd at first to write a "to-don't" list, but it also helps clarify your purpose and mission.

It's good to be aspirational, but you have to be true to who you are. Authenticity matters, and pretending to be someone else rarely works. As Sam Fiorello from Cortex told us, "You're not going to out-Austin, Austin." Each city, anchor institution, and innovation district is unique.

Rather than building from scratch, start with whatever you have and find ways to strengthen it.

Plan for Inclusion and Equity

Use an equity lens to think through the decisions you're making, and consider how they will affect the community in a year, a decade, or a century. As we discussed in chapter 10, part of that forward thinking is being aware of unintended consequences. For example, institutions typically grow, and the most common way is to acquire land on the periphery. But this cycle tends to destabilize neighborhoods, causing people to speculate on the land (geographer Neil Smith wrote about predicting gentrification by using the "rent gap," which is the difference between the potential rent and the actual rent).[1] So one of the first things we did in Buffalo was decide to concentrate development in the core of the innovation district. We haven't always strictly adhered to this plan, but we're keenly aware of the potential problems when we don't.

At every stage of the planning process, ask yourself questions like, "What effect will this have on families experiencing poverty?" or "Is this equitable for people who are transgender?" Every plan has consequences, so consider what those will be for people who are older, disabled, or experiencing homelessness. As always, I encourage you to take a broad view of equity throughout your community.

At the Buffalo Niagara Medical Campus (BNMC), we developed our MutualCity framework (see the Appendix) to guide our firm belief that our success is intrinsically linked to progress in the community. In just a few short sentences, MutualCity outlines what we believe are the most effective principles for advancing equity. That said, we formulated these principles years after we published our master plan in 2003. We wrote about equity-related concepts in the master plan ("In building the future prosperity of Buffalo, we can leave no one out"), but we never actually used the word *equity*. I can make excuses and say it's because the word (and the concept) wasn't widely in play at the time, but really it was a blind spot and an oversight on our part, and we continue to take steps to correct it.

If you're just starting out, plan for inclusion and equity from the beginning in order to establish it as a core value. If you don't prioritize it—and back that up with a clear strategy, as well as the money and people to do the work—it's always going to be an afterthought, and you'll struggle to make progress.

Even if you're an established organization, you can still embed these values in your governance and plans. Hire a director of equity. Establish an equity committee (with the same power and influence as your other committees, of course). Update your master plan to include equity-related goals for the community. Later is better than never.

Recognize that advancing equity takes more time and effort than ignoring it. Temper your expectations, be patient, and let others know what you can—and can't—plan to achieve. Systemic issues don't get resolved overnight. Be optimistic but also realistic.

It's easy to talk a good game and make bold proclamations about equity and inclusion, then forget about those parts of the plan when it's time to execute. But good intentions alone don't help people. A plan is a waste of time, effort, and paper if you can't execute on it. Think about what you're truly committing to in your plan and whether you're ready to take on that responsibility. If not, then be clear about when you might be.

Be Proactive

You can't plan for everything. But the more you're thinking about the issues that affect your community, the better position you'll be in.

Being proactive about equity saves lives in a crisis. "'We may be the only community in the country that's been able to mute the impact of this pandemic, and that's directly attributable to the work we did with our university partners that started in previous years,'" said Kinzer Pointer, a member of our Better Together pastor group and co-convener of the African American Health Equity Task Force, which has collaborated with the University at Buffalo and Buffalo Center for Health Equity to develop a more effective response to the pandemic.[2] Thanks in large part to their ongoing, coordinated efforts to help address health disparities throughout our community, African Americans in Buffalo are proportionately much less likely to die from COVID-19 than those in other communities nationwide.

Consider the Timing

Understand the seasons and cycles that affect your partners. Elected officials may be more receptive to plans during their first year in office, before the pressure of reelection. Hospitals, universities, and other organizations often go through months-long accreditation processes every several years (up to about ten years), drawing significant time and attention from leaders and staff. Retail and restaurant partners may have seasonal lulls, especially in college towns where students head home for summer and breaks. These issues affect not only when you'll be able to collaborate with partners on creating a plan but also the timing of executing the plan itself.

Don't wait for the perfect time, or until it's too late. There is no perfect time, and there's often no reason to wait. If you're planning to fight for racial equity a year from now, why wouldn't you start today? Even if you don't have all the resources you need right now, surely there's something you can do to get started.

Remember that bold deadlines inspire action. Yes, they may seem audacious and unachievable at first. But—again, back to the "five whys"—once you start digging in and asking why you can't do it, you'll often find that many of the obstacles are purely psychological.

Take a long-term view. One hundred years into the future isn't that far when you're thinking about issues such as climate change. But remember to look to the past, too. Walk into any city hall or sizable organization and you're likely to find shelves filled with dusty binders of plans that never came to be. Yet even plans that were tossed aside often have a few gems inside them. Spend a morning reading through plans that never came to fruition and you may be surprised by what you can put into action today.

Find a Mirror

When you put your head down and get to work, you can get a lot done, but you don't always see the big picture strategy or the impact you're having. It helps to get an outside perspective when you need one—someone to hold up a mirror and show you what you're doing right and where there's room for improvement.

Shortly after we founded the BNMC, we connected with the Heron foundation—a New York City–based foundation with a reputation for championing change. Our staff had basically doubled in a year and half, and we needed help managing the internal growth rather than basically just duct-taping it together. Dana Bezerra and her talented team at Heron helped us create a business plan, but perhaps more importantly they showed us how much we had already accomplished and pointed out that nobody else was doing the type of work we were doing. That insight helped us see we were on the right track and gave us the confidence to keep taking on new challenges.

When Are You Done?

"The completion of the master plan document does not signal an end to the campus planning effort," we wrote in our master plan. The planning process never truly ends.

We were extremely fortunate that the BNMC met its growth trajectories from our master plan in just six years and that we had to update our plan at that time. (It's important to note, however, that our plan was focused primarily on physical and economic growth; in subsequent updates and documents, we've been more deliberate about cultivating a shared vision with the community.)

It's especially important to keep moving forward once you've achieved your initial goals. "Sometimes, people start to think, 'OK, it's been a success, we don't really have to pay attention to the campus anymore, now we can go back and think about our silos again,'" said Bill Joyce, former chair of the BNMC board of directors. The best way to keep people engaged is to always be planning for what comes next, especially as your organization matures.

As an innovation district, we'll always need to think about basics like parking and safety. That's BNMC 1.0, as I call it. But what is our potential to effect even greater change throughout the community? How can we use what we've built these past twenty years—the facilities, programs, and connections—to advance equity throughout the city for the next twenty years and beyond? Initiatives like EforAll are part of this effort, but it's going to take people coming back to the table, probably getting a little uncomfortable (just like we were in the beginning), and using the social design process to identify problems. And so the cycle begins again.

A Flexible Framework

My former boss, Rick Reinhard, used to say that when you create a plan, you hope that 25 percent of it happens. You don't have a crystal ball. When you try to predict the future, you're probably going to get something—maybe a lot of things—wrong.

Cities are constantly reshaping themselves. The social design process is intentionally dynamic and open to ever-changing inputs. People are unpredictable. All of which means that you have to accept uncertainty. Coastal cities like Miami now have to plan for things like climate gentrification, in which homes are worth more if they're in neighborhoods that are on higher ground.[3] Climate change is an issue that wasn't even on the radar just a few decades ago but is now a critical factor in designing more equitable cities.

When my family takes road trips, we'll map out the route but also plan for detours and stops. You have to be open to deviation from your plan—whether it's a forced deviation or one you chose—given the fast-moving nature of many equity-related issues. If you're not nimble and open to changing your plans, you're going to be frustrated, and you're going to miss out on opportunities.

In today's world, a flexible framework creates an environment that allows everyone to participate and engage—especially as circumstances evolve. One thing that I think has helped the BNMC is that we're not a very formal organization. We don't have a lot of layers. We'll talk to almost anyone, anytime, about anything that affects the community, which has led to some amazing partnerships and collaborations. We know that our organization doesn't have all the answers. None of us do. But together, we can find a better way.

The Importance of Leadership

Planning and pivoting both take leadership. I talk with so many people who want to be successful, grow their organization, and have a positive impact on the community. But those things don't just happen by themselves. I see it all the time with organizations that don't fully realize how important leadership is, how hard it is, and how much work it really takes. You need a leader who will take a stand, make tough decisions, set the direction, and then actually lead people on that path. You can have the best plan in the world, but if your leadership isn't effective, you're not going to get very far. I've talked a lot about leadership in this book, but I strongly encourage you to consider how it fits into your planning process—including a plan for how you're going to attract, retain, and grow leaders within your organization.

Be Open to Serendipity

When the Robert Wood Johnson Foundation provided a grant to make our innovation district more walkable, we planted trees, fixed sidewalks, and installed lights. Then one day they asked whether we wanted money to work on food ecosystems, too. "Of course we do!" I quickly replied, not having any idea how we were going to do it. But we figured it out. We hired someone, thanks to support from the local Community Foundation. We partnered with one of the leading food resiliency experts in the world. And with our newfound knowledge, we earned a grant through the U.S. Department of Agriculture to do even more.

When I look at all of our accomplishments now, it was never our original goal to tackle many of them. We just didn't have the vision, or the resources, at first. But we had a solid foundation, we were flexible, and we were willing to try just about anything. There's a lot to be said for simply being in the right place at the right time. Be open to chance meetings, opportune timing, and serendipitous events. As painter Bob Ross would say, embrace the "happy little accidents."[4]

I got this job in part because of serendipity. Rick Reinhard, who was hired to do the original feasibility study of the medical campus, happened to work across the street from my father-in-law's best friend, Tom Beecher. (Reinhard was known for starting a concert series in Buffalo that lasted nearly thirty years and attracted Bo Diddley, Buffalo's own Goo Goo Dolls, and other musical stars.) Reinhard told Beecher he needed to hire someone, and Beecher recommended me. I was in the right place at the right time.

Of course, it wasn't just serendipity. You have to work hard and put yourself in a position to take advantage of opportunities when they pop up. But I also know that I was there—in that place, at that time—in part because of the advantages I have. I'm a White man from a middle-class suburban family. My wife's family knew Beecher, who was one of the most well-known businesspeople in the city at that time. I say this not to apologize for my good fortune but to acknowledge that it was not just serendipity and hard work that put me in this position.

When Opportunity Knocks

In St. Paul, Minnesota, the Public Works department stamps poems into the concrete when repairing broken sidewalks. They've done so many that now everyone in the city lives within a ten-minute walk of one of these Sidewalk Poems.[5] Think about ways you can leverage work that's already being done, repurpose building materials, or even carve out a park from underused land. Look for ways to improve equity or quality of life with everything you do.

Think beyond infrastructure and how you can tap into all of the resources around you. In our innovation district, there's a university that's one of the top 1 percent in the world. We've partnered with their faculty, staff, and students on countless projects, and we'd be remiss not to. Our member institutions include the largest healthcare provider in the region, a state-of-the-art hearing and speech center, and the world's first cancer research center. I can walk down the hall—or up the street—and meet with scientists, engineers, marketers, and other experts from dozens of startup companies on campus. Chances are you're also surrounded by experts. How can they add insight, perspective, and authority to your projects and help you achieve your goals? Wander around your organization or campus, and you may be surprised what you can learn.

Serendipity is why many organizations choose to be part of an innovation district. You never know who you'll meet walking from the subway station, lining up for a food truck, or grabbing a hot cup of coffee.

You may discover the perfect hire, find a funder for your startup, or even overhear information about a new business opportunity. If you're designing infrastructure and programs and projects, create them with serendipity in mind. Just as Nick Hopkins envisioned a building that forces "collisions" between people, you can apply this concept to your buildings, policies, and processes and spark the perfect conditions for serendipity to occur.

Planning and Flexibility in a Crisis

When a crisis hits—and it will—having a solid plan and the ability to be flexible can easily be the difference between whether your organization survives or not.

As I mentioned at the beginning of this chapter, the start of the COVID-19 pandemic completely changed the way we work. We kept our master plan but had to rethink our entire business model. Innovation districts are deliberately designed to bring people together, so when a virus stopped us from meeting and mingling in person, it turned our business model upside down.

Think about how a crisis will change things not only in the moment but also in the long term. In the days and weeks immediately after the terrorist attacks of September 11, 2001, in the United States, we saw stringent new security practices in place at airports and on planes. Twenty years later, those precautions (and others) are still in effect. During the COVID-19 pandemic, millions of people started working from home. My bet is that they won't all be working from home in a few years—but they won't all be back at the office, either.

Consider the emotional impact of a crisis and how it leaves many of us anxious and worried, often for years to come. For those who lost a loved one or friend, the scars are even deeper. Empathy matters more than ever.

Understand how a crisis can exacerbate inequities. During the COVID-19 pandemic, masks became ubiquitous, creating a hurdle for people with hearing impairments, who may rely on reading lips. Many students in low-income communities struggled with online classes, because of slow internet speeds and conditions at home. You should already be looking for these inequities in your work, but pay extra attention in times of crisis.

If there's a silver lining, it's that a crisis can also force you to embrace the future, perhaps sooner than you would have otherwise. In California, one city transitioned to paperless permits in a month instead of a year.[6] Rapid change gives you a window of time in which you can quickly reshape, reform, and rebuild—ideally with equity in mind. "History shows time and again that once recovery resources are allocated, the best a city can usually hope for is to get back to some kind of pre-disaster 'normal,'" wrote Felicia Henry and Scott Gabriel Knowles. "But what if 'normal' in your community before the pandemic was a day-to-day disaster of injustice: Structural racism and violence, health inequality, failing schools and low-paying jobs, and environmental hazards? No city in America, especially Philadelphia with the highest poverty rate among American cities, is going to come out of the pandemic better than before unless we radically alter our conception of disaster recovery."[7]

Why settle for what you had before, when that clearly wasn't good enough? If you have the right plan in place, and you're able to be flexible, it's easier to keep equity at the forefront as you manage a crisis.

Conclusion and On the Horizon

In 1881, Buffalo was one of the first cities in the United States to have electric streetlights, thanks to cheap hydropower from nearby Niagara Falls.

The problem was that more than a century later, some of that same electric infrastructure was still being used in the city. As one utility executive said only partially in jest, "Thomas Edison himself touched the wires you have in your system."[1]

Our ancient electric grid couldn't support Buffalo's fast-growing hospitals and research institutions. So we talked with the electric utility and developed a strategy that addressed the needs of the anchor institutions. But we didn't stop there.

We met with residents of the adjacent neighborhood and found that lowering their electric bills even by just a few dollars a month could make a significant, tangible, and immediate difference in a community where nearly half of the residents were living in poverty.

Solar panels seemed like the right solution, but many residents had low credit scores and income levels that didn't allow them to receive solar panel tax credits. So we partnered with the electric utility (National Grid) and New York State to install solar panels on 100 rooftops throughout the adjacent neighborhood, all at no cost to homeowners.

This program didn't reverse the effects of redlining, abolish income inequity, or eliminate systemic racism. It just helped a number of people living in a low-income area gain access to an opportunity that their wealthier neighbors already had. But it was one of the first projects that showed our commitment to equity and proved that we could make a real impact in the community if we worked together.

☼ ☼ ☼

My first job was working for Lorne Michaels at *Saturday Night Live*. I made popcorn for him, and once I stopped burning his popcorn, I got more responsibilities. I've burned plenty of popcorn over the years—literally and figuratively. But with the help of countless people here in Buffalo and far beyond, we've had plenty of successes, too. I'm proud to say we've done more than most, even if it's still not enough.

Here's my advice: Don't get discouraged. You're going to burn some popcorn. You're going to run into obstacles. People will tell you that your plans won't work. City Hall will put up red tape. You won't have enough money, or time, or people. That's okay. You can still do *something*. Find one thing that's inequitable and make it better. Even just planting one tree can replace the need for ten air conditioners.[2] But you have to start somewhere. Nobody else is going to solve your city's problems.

When you get frustrated—and you will—remember the lessons from this book.

Steal shamelessly. Know when to take the back seat. Build bridges. Find ideas that are good for most of the people.

And keep moving your city forward.

On the Horizon

"What's next?" It's a question I ask every day. Because if all you do is focus on what you did yesterday, you're going to get crushed by tomorrow. There are new opportunities to discover and new challenges to deal with in every corner of your community. You can't ignore them. You have to face them head-on and understand that the actions you take today will have consequences. So are you going to make life better or worse for people in your community? And will it be better for *everyone*, or just for some people? That's what I hope you'll keep in mind as you think about the future.

The Future of Cities

Let's start with some basic demographics. By 2044, White people will be a minority in the United States as a whole.[3] White people are already a minority in many cities, but they still often lead (or have significant influence on) the city's government, large businesses, and most powerful institutions.[4] Immigration, though subject to ever-evolving legislation, still affects our cities, contributing to nearly 90 percent of population growth in some metro areas.[5] As political differences continue to divide our country, there is potential for immigrants, minorities, and other underserved populations to become further disenfranchised. Anchor institutions and innovation districts can help counter this trend by working closely with these groups, protecting their voices, serving their communities, and highlighting their unique contributions to our cities. In Buffalo, for example, our innovation district hires immigrants and refugees and trains them for careers.

Nationwide, our population will continue to age, but the average age of city residents typically remains a few years younger than the national average. Millennials (born 1981–1996) and Gen Z (born 1997–2012) are increasingly important groups, in terms of both their numbers and their views on equity. For example, unlike Baby Boomers, a majority of Gen Z and Millennials believe that more racial and ethnic diversity is good for society.[6] Gen Z and Millennials are much more likely to know someone who prefers gender-neutral pronouns. Equity matters more to

Gen Z and Millennials than it does to older generations, and we expect to see younger generations follow this trend. We should also consider the extraordinary impact of "influencers" in sports, music, and popular culture. As these influencers mature (and new ones arise), we expect that they will demand more diversity in our culture, our elected officials, and our communities—which will help put a spotlight on equity-related issues. Influencers can also help us build bridges with the community; in Buffalo, we're partnering with a well-known rapper to redesign the space in the Innovation Center to make it more appealing to people throughout the city.

As cities expand out instead of up (some estimates show a potential increase of 80 percent in global urban land area by 2030), the poorest residents may face even greater inequality—including longer and more expensive commutes—as they are forced to "drive until you qualify" to find affordable housing.[7] (And yes, anchors and innovation districts can exacerbate this trend through development, as discussed in previous chapters.) Poverty is still concentrated in our cities but is a growing problem in the suburbs. Even as some groups move out, others are moving into certain neighborhoods; here in Buffalo, we expect to see our residential population continue to rise downtown, fueled in part by older people who want the convenience, access to healthcare, and other amenities of living in a city.

Although big cities will remain attractive, the COVID-19 pandemic will probably cause some to seek less densely populated areas, especially if more people are able to work from home on a permanent basis. "It used to be that you went to where the job was. Now the job is coming to you," said Tom Osha, board chair of The Global Institute on Innovation Districts and senior vice president at Wexford Science & Technology. This may be advantageous to smaller cities (some of which have actively lured remote workers), but it can also cause a strain in housing prices, school enrollment, and overall city services.

Aside from a small number of cities that are doing well financially, most cities are struggling to sustain themselves and are trying to do more with less. As a result, anchors and innovation districts are increasingly being called upon to help fill the gap. In Buffalo, our innovation district helped create the region's first mobility hub to encourage cost-effective, climate-friendly commuting. In the past, this type of regional effort probably would have been led by the government. Moving forward, as underfunded cities grapple with evolving short-term and long-term threats, anchors and innovation districts have an opportunity (and, I would argue, a responsibility) to take on proactive leadership roles typically filled by government.

It's important to recognize that, whether handled by innovation districts or cities, equity-related projects don't have to be costly. In Buffalo, we offer microgrants for our neighbors to further improve the quality of life; recent projects include a sensory garden for the blind and visually impaired and a program that helps students manage stress through poetry and art. As you look ahead, remember that achieving a greater social impact often relies more on your perspective and ingenuity than your budget.

Thankfully, we expect more cities to formally recognize the importance of equity and further prioritize equity as a consideration in their decision making. Even gestures like renaming part of one of Buffalo's busiest streets as Black Lives Matter Way are welcome steps toward a stronger community (although, to be clear, renaming a street is simply a show of support and doesn't actually move the needle on equity). One promising metric is the rising number of chief equity officers—"a new kind of CEO"—primarily in large and more progressive cities but a soon-to-be requirement for other cities throughout the country.[8] These officials identify inequities throughout the community and help people in local government recognize and address gaps in order to advance equity. Although the practice of having someone in this leadership position dates back at least to the early 2000s with Seattle's Office of Civil Rights, many universities have had diversity officers for much longer.[9]

The Future of Anchor Institutions and Innovation Districts

Innovation districts are now an established (and often expected) feature of thriving cities. Everybody wants one, which is why they're popping up across the country. As I write this, at least a dozen new ones are in the works, including many in smaller cities such as Ithaca, New York; Pompano Beach, Florida; and Broken Arrow, Oklahoma. As one innovation district leader called them, they are the "shiny new object" that every city and developer wants in their portfolio, just as entertainment districts were in the 1980s.

In the past, the anchors populating these innovation districts have typically been hospitals, universities, and cultural institutions. Moving forward, we expect to see greater interest and engagement from flagship corporations, startup companies, community organizations, and others who want to make a greater impact on their city. I also think we'll see more foundations emerge as "a new kind of anchor institution," as the Cleveland Foundation is doing by embracing local neighborhoods and moving into an innovation district.[10] At the Buffalo Niagara Medical Campus, we've gladly provided much-needed space and other valuable resources to local nonprofits, startup companies, and EforAll and eforever (which you read about in chapter 10).

That said, even traditional anchor institutions are evolving. A few days after my daughter had her wisdom teeth removed, she had some lingering pain. Sitting in the waiting room of the dentist's office, I wondered: How long will it be before video chats will replace packed waiting rooms? How long before distance learning replaces university lecture halls? For centuries, anchor institutions have needed cavernous buildings and parking garages. In the not-so-distant future—thanks to technology (and accelerated by the COVID-19 pandemic)—many of these facilities may be more of a costly hindrance than anything else. It's happening with shopping malls, and I doubt that hospitals and universities are far behind. In many cases, we don't need to replicate the *experience* (of going to the doctor, for example) to achieve the same *results*—although, as we saw during COVID-19, any digital solutions need to be thoughtfully considered, especially in terms of their impact on those who cannot access technology as intended.

In the future, more employees who work in anchor institutions and innovation districts will probably be working from home, co-working spaces, and other remote locations due to technological advances, the increasing difficulty of commuting, or public health epidemics that require social distancing. Regardless of where employees will be working, consider what types of jobs will be needed in the future and how they will affect equity in your community. For example, the fastest-growing occupations with the largest number of employees also have the lowest salaries—40 percent less than the next-lowest-paying job.[11]

The gig economy will probably have a growing impact on anchors and innovation districts. Nurses are already working with staffing companies and using smartphone apps to create their own schedules.[12] In terms of terms of equity, however, gig workers often earn lower pay, don't typically get sick time or health insurance, and have "jobs" that are less predictable and stable.

From a financial standpoint, at least in the immediate aftermath of COVID-19, hospitals are facing unprecedented losses, many universities are bracing for lower enrollment and reduced research funding, and companies (especially startups) are struggling. Some startup companies and small businesses will surely thrive, but many will probably be constrained, at least in the short term, by a lack of capital.

Although I believe that innovation districts will come back stronger than ever, at times the pandemic made me question their future. Many core advantages of an innovation district—including density, proximity, and an environment that promotes spontaneity—were liabilities during COVID-19. So we'll keep reevaluating how we bring people together and be more aware of how we include people who are immunocompromised or homebound.

The good news is that many people are now increasingly aware of (and thankful for) anchor institutions and innovation districts and their contributions to society through research, health care, and countless other areas. Whether we're talking about addressing climate change, curing cancer, or tackling nearly any of society's most intimidating challenges, there are people hard at work solving these problems at anchor institutions and in innovation districts around the world. I'm hopeful that governments and other funders will provide a level of support that reflects the innumerable benefits that innovation districts offer.

Remember that innovation districts are a new phenomenon. Unlike universities and museums that may be hundreds of years old, even the earliest innovation districts have been around only for decades. Given our limited history, it's difficult to predict what will happen, especially in terms of job pipelines and other initiatives that could take many years to fully materialize.

The Next Wave of Collaboration

With a growing number of innovation districts—and more collaboration between anchor institutions—there are even more opportunities for us to work together and learn from each other, locally, regionally, nationally, and globally. We're seeing more articles about innovation districts (even in mainstream media), and more resources and groups to serve them, including The Global Institute on Innovation Districts, which we helped establish as a founding member.

For years, most anchor institutions and innovation districts have worked closely with traditional partners, including governments, foundations, and nonprofit organizations. Expect to see new governance and organizational models for innovation districts emerging. In some cases, the government will be heavily involved (especially outside the United States). In other communities, we're more likely to see nonprofit organizations, university-led collaborations, or public–private partnerships at the helm of new or revitalized innovation districts.

In the future, we'll probably see a continued rise in the influence of corporate partners specializing in services for anchors and innovation districts; these partners include real estate developers, financiers, and companies that manage co-working space. There's certainly value to gaining expertise from these types of corporations, and it's possible that these partnerships will free innovation districts to focus more on equity-related efforts. But I encourage you to consider all the implications of these corporate partnerships—including, for example, how an anchor's relationship with a for-profit, publicly traded investor affects the anchor's commitment to improving equity for everyone in the community.

Beyond corporate partners, I believe that anchors and innovation districts will continue to engage more consistently and productively with a much broader range of grassroots community groups, activists, and others who are on the front lines of creating more equitable cities—or have the potential to do so. Inspired by Black Lives Matter and other social justice movements, we'll see organizations striving to be more diverse and inclusive—not just in terms of how people look but in terms of how they think and everything they have to offer. I hope that we can lead by example as anchor institutions and innovation districts open their doors, literally and figuratively, to welcome more people in and take a more intentional approach. This won't be easy; after all, most businesses are accustomed to making widgets and then selling those widgets. Their purpose isn't to care about social justice. But why can't companies make money *and* make society more equitable? That's where, as an innovation district, we can help open people's eyes to the possibilities. Fortunately, this gets easier every year, as younger generations eager for change enter the workforce.

Finally, consider how ever-evolving communication platforms will continue to influence the ways we collaborate and share information. Online videos, text messages, and social media are the communication vehicles of choice for younger generations—at least for those who have internet access (which certainly isn't a given when you're working with underserved communities). You don't always need to be on the cutting edge—an email newsletter might be perfect for more conventional audiences such as municipalities—but I'd encourage you to review your communication strategies and platforms at least once a year and ensure that they're aligned with how your various audiences are receiving and sharing information.

The Future of Equitable Cities

Based on our unique perspective and expertise in creating more equitable communities for the past twenty years, here are a few more trends and predictions related to equitable cities, along with examples of how anchor institutions and innovation districts are already leading by example and laying the groundwork for addressing future challenges.

Climate Change and Green Gentrification

Expect climate change to have a monumental impact on your city. Even here in Buffalo with our moderate year-round temperatures, I am increasingly concerned about potential heat waves, flooding, and other extreme climate events. Climate change affects everyone, but its impact is often disproportionately felt by lower-income people.

As you plan for climate change in your city, think about who is most at risk, today and in the future. Poorly built houses will not stand up to extreme storms. Low-lying communities will be the first to be flooded from rising seas. Anchor institutions and innovation districts can take the lead by being aware of these trends and by taking steps to combat climate change, such as mandating roof gardens, which can cut heat flow through the roof in the spring and summer by up to 75 percent.[13]

Access to Water and Other Resources

Clean, fresh water will be an increasingly scarce resource. By 2040, for example, "demand for water will exceed supply in Raleigh."[14] Whether shortages are driven by rising populations or by poor decision making (as we've seen with lead pipes in Flint, Michigan), the effects are often disproportionately felt by lower-income communities, in which residents can't afford to move or purchase bottled water.

Food Security

Advances in food technology, including plant-based meat replacements, may help feed more people, but it will be difficult to keep pace with the world's growing population. Indoor vertical farms show promise and are an attractive solution for cities looking to repurpose buildings, but they often depend on affordable rent and the ability to compete with conventional farms, which can be highly subsidized. Climate change will continue to affect growing patterns and will also keep pushing climate refugees to new homes, where they may not have the land or conditions needed to grow culturally appropriate foods. Given the impact of food on nearly every aspect of a person's life—and the disproportionate effect of food insecurity on people of color—I'm hopeful that cities, anchor institutions, and innovation districts will focus more on food systems and take advantage of what Samina Raja calls "the power of the food system to connect to broader social problems such as poverty."[15]

Technology

I was walking through Manhattan with my daughter when we saw a sign on the door of a restaurant: "No cash accepted." Sure, we could use a credit card or an app on my phone to pay the bill. But what about the man experiencing homelessness who we passed along the way, with his handful of dollar bills? What about the refugee who doesn't have a credit card? New York City has banned cashless businesses, recognizing that they excluded some of their most marginalized residents.

As technology keeps moving forward, we must keep pace in our thinking about how it affects equity, beyond the digital divide. For example, as schools use artificial intelligence (AI) to grade papers and create lesson plans, will AI reduce or exacerbate equity gaps in education? As "smart cities" use technology to automate traffic flow, will it benefit drivers at the expense of pedestrian safety? How could technology such as facial recognition be used to discriminate against ethnic groups? The impact will depend largely on who is in control of the technology and what they prioritize, which is why it will be increasingly important for everyone to have a voice in how this new technology is developed and applied, even (and perhaps especially) in the technologies we can't see.

Finally, in terms of technology, I'm hopeful that our increasingly digital world will include a renewed focus on placemaking and other initiatives that promote real-life human interactions.

Shopping

Online shopping will continue to increase, threatening the future of local retail (including perhaps retail stores in and around innovation districts) and the livelihood of millions of retail employees, as well as those involved in the supply chain. But online shopping does more than strip away local jobs. It dehumanizes the exchange of goods, disconnects us even further from manufacturers, and can increase pollution and congestion in cities suddenly clogged with heavy-duty delivery trucks. The Los Angeles Cleantech Incubator is exploring options to solve the transportation issues, including using central facilities as distribution centers, then using last-mile delivery options such as e-bikes to reduce traffic in the city.[16]

Energy and Fuel Poverty

Energy is one of the most important topics we can talk about in terms of equity and the future. Low-income households have an energy burden three times higher than that of non–low-income households.[17] "Black and Hispanic-majority census tracts" have fewer rooftop solar panels, even when we account for racial differences in income and other factors.[18] Energy affects our health, as continued use of fossil fuels leads to air pollution and contributes to climate change. We often take energy for granted, especially in the United States—but without it, society comes to a standstill.

Rising energy costs can lead to fuel poverty, in which households cannot afford (or spend a disproportionate amount of their income on) the energy needed for heating, transportation, and other daily functions. Given the volatility in energy prices, it's difficult to predict whether this will be a growing problem in the future; however, one way to mitigate these concerns is by continuing to transition to renewable energy, especially in communities that would be most affected by rising energy costs.

Unfortunately, many people underestimate the cost of switching from fossil fuels to renewable energy. Solar and wind farms are often located many miles from cities, which means you have to pay for solar panels and turbines and then spend millions (or billions) more to upgrade the distribution system that carries the energy to cities. And if too many households and organizations switch to electric heat and transportation (charging electric vehicles at home, for example), our existing distribution systems at the neighborhood level simply won't be able to handle the demand.

So what's the solution? Here in Buffalo, we have a history of being at the forefront of energy innovation, thanks in part to Nikola Tesla, whose vision for AC current helped engineers harness power from nearby Niagara Falls in the late 1800s. Today, a Buffalo-based company, Viridi Parente, is using a distributed energy model to provide competitively priced renewable energy.[19] (Led by Jon Williams, the company is also working on green excavators that use batteries and motors instead of diesel engines.)

I'm one of Viridi Parente's test subjects, which means I'll get a large battery in my home, hooked up to my main electric line. During off-peak hours (when there's less demand for electricity and it costs less to buy it), we'll charge the battery. Then we'll use this stored electricity from the battery during peak hours. This system puts less strain on the electric grid, saves us money, and even allows us to sell electricity back to the utility.

Right now, cost is a major barrier to implementing this distributed approach. But imagine if, instead of spending billions of dollars on solar and wind farms and upgraded distribution systems, we spent that money to manufacture and install these types of small-scale, location-based energy systems that could work cost-effectively in any neighborhood. Viridi Parente is testing this approach at Northland Workforce Training Center in Buffalo, which will feature a microgrid with a battery storage system and locally based renewable energy. The site will be a living lab, where people can study how to implement this approach in cities throughout the country.

"You have to get away from setting goals, and focus on the problem you need to solve," says Dennis Elsenbeck, president of Viridi Parente, echoing a key principle of social design. The company's model also aligns energy innovation with economic development by providing financial incentives for everyone involved, from governments and utilities to the end users. In the coming years, I'm interested in seeing how this approach works for the community and whether it can be expanded in Buffalo and replicated in other cities.

Gender Inequality

Discrimination against women and girls still exists, and too few women are in leadership positions—including in our own organization. Looking forward, I expect to see more grassroots efforts such as the #MeToo movement, which helped shine a spotlight on sexual harassment and assault. From an institutional standpoint, achieving gender equality remains one of the United Nations' Sustainable Development Goals and should be considered in your efforts to create a more equitable city, from planning safe public spaces to offering gender-inclusive programming.

Education

In 2020, we saw massive disruption in education as the COVID-19 virus shut down schools and universities around the world. Although remote learning had gained some traction previously, especially with a handful of online-focused universities, the global pandemic meant that millions of students went from sitting in a classroom to sitting in front of a screen in a matter of weeks. We probably won't know for years the full impact of this shift to online learning, although it's clear that remote learning, in part because of inequitable access to Wi-Fi, will disproportionately affect lower-income learners, the disabled, and those with special educational needs.

Healthcare

As we discussed earlier in this chapter, I expect that telehealth will gain greater footholds in the healthcare industry, eliminating some of the need for massive brick-and-mortar facilities. Some of the fastest-growing jobs are in healthcare, but they're also typically low-paid positions, which may not be as effective in closing the equity gap. Perhaps the most notable future developments will result from the COVID-19 pandemic, which magnified (especially for the public) many of the flaws in our current healthcare system, from the insurance providers to disease testing to hospital capacity. In the future, I believe that organizations will become better equipped to address inequities in healthcare (including racial disparities in treatment), allowing them to be more intentional about the way they deliver care to all.

Transportation

The percentage of electric vehicles on our streets will continue to rise. I'm proud to say that the Buffalo Niagara Medical Campus has always been at the forefront regionally in terms of providing charging stations for electric vehicles and currently has one of the largest concentrations of electric vehicle charging stations in New York State. Adoption in low-income areas will continue to lag behind because of high upfront costs.

The shift to autonomous vehicles should provide significant savings in terms of time, money, space, and other resources. Cities will be able to have narrower roads and fewer parking spots, which currently take up 40–60 percent of the space in many cities.[20] Although some experts think that autonomous vehicles may actually *increase* traffic (as time in a car becomes more productive), I'm hopeful that technology will allow for more vehicular density, thus offsetting any rise in traffic.

As always, equity should be at the forefront of the conversation. As the rise of autonomous vehicles (hopefully) leads to less demand for large parking structures, anchors and innovation districts can help ensure that everyone in the community benefits from the available land in prime downtown areas. Autonomous vehicles that prioritize the safety of pedestrians and cyclists could help drastically reduce injuries and deaths among these groups. We must also consider opportunities for autonomous vehicles to serve older adults, the disabled, and other marginalized groups.[21]

If more people continue to work from home, we may continue to see improved air quality, fewer pedestrian deaths, and other benefits of fewer vehicles (especially gas-powered vehicles) on the roads.

As we look at public transportation, we see some cities raising fares, whereas cities such as Kansas City, Missouri, are offering public transportation for free, resulting in an immediate rise in ridership and providing a critical step toward creating equitable communities.[22] Anchors and innovation districts are often hubs (and therefore advocates) for public transportation and will continue to be so in the future. However, as cities are faced with maintaining aging subway and light rail systems, more cost-effective systems such as bus rapid transit will probably take hold in more metro areas.

Ridesharing will probably increase in popularity, which may provide more access to transportation but leaves out those who don't have a smartphone and often relies on gig economy drivers who may be subject to lower pay and less stability. I see promise in micromobility (including the bikes and scooters that are ubiquitous in some cities), especially given that these are low-cost, typically low-polluting options. However, to date, micromobility solutions have typically focused on upper-income men rather than taking a more inclusive approach.[23]

Financial Systems and Economic Impact
In the future, a growing number of community development loan funds could help address appraisal gaps (situations in which the appraisal is lower than the amount of funds it would take to develop a property), clearing the way for more affordable housing and development in underserved neighborhoods. Banking systems are also evolving; in California, for example, cities can now create their own public banks, which should help promote affordable housing via lower-interest loans to public agencies. Unfortunately, the finance industry is still an old boys' club in many ways. Of all the registered asset management firms in

the United States, minority- and women-owned (MWO) firms manage less than 1 percent of the assets, despite the fact that their performance is comparable to that of non-MWO firms.[24] Although I hope to see this change—especially with the influx of newer generations to the profession—I don't think the industry will evolve as quickly as it should. In Buffalo, we're addressing this issue in part by inviting a diverse group of people from throughout the community to learn about investing by helping to manage one of our funds. (Of course, we also benefit, as they teach us more about the community-wide needs.)

Cities, companies, and other organizations will continue to use economic impact in making decisions about development, budget allocation, and key initiatives. However, these groups will increasingly focus on the social impact of their actions and will be more likely (and more empowered) to make decisions that help address equity gaps. For example, in St. Louis, banks that want to hold municipal deposits are now asked to share diversity data and information about how they are serving unbanked and underbanked communities.[25]

Housing

The cost of housing in cities will probably continue to rise, driven by everything from population growth and short-term rentals to increasing scarcity of units. Increasing costs will probably continue to push more and more people out to the suburbs, where housing may be more affordable, but with the trade-off of longer commutes and fewer services. Many innovation districts—recognizing that they contribute to rising housing costs, especially in their communities—are including housing units in future development plans and will continue to offer financial incentives for innovation district employees who live in the surrounding areas. In Buffalo, our innovation district supports the Fruit Belt Community Land Trust, which works to create "homes that remain permanently affordable, providing successful homeownership opportunities to lower-income families for generations to come."[26]

Given that housing costs are, by far, the largest portion of a typical resident's annual expenditures (and disproportionately high for low-income residents), any significant changes in housing costs will affect residents' ability to pay for other basic needs. Beyond the cost of rent and mortgages, aging housing stocks (especially in many northeastern cities such as Buffalo) will continue to burden homeowners and renters who struggle to heat poorly insulated homes during harsh winters.

In the future, I believe we'll see a greater push for more sustainable housing solutions, more co-living opportunities for seniors, and increasing demand for homes in walkable neighborhoods.

Finally, the number of people experiencing homelessness continues to rise—quite sharply in many cities. As nonprofit organizations such as Community Solutions continue to advocate and change lives nationwide, I hope that anchor institutions and innovation districts will pay more attention to this issue and work together on a comprehensive approach.

An Uncertain Future

"The only lasting truth is Change," wrote Octavia Butler.[27] Before 2020, few could have predicted that COVID-19 would destroy lives, upend economies, and transform societies around the world. On a less somber note, we've seen new technologies and platforms such as ridesharing, social media, and the gig economy disrupt entire industries—and we're sure to see it again. The only question is when it will happen. We must be prepared for change, however (and whenever) it arrives. Complacency kills. You have to keep looking forward. You may be surprised by *what* comes next—but you won't be caught off guard by the countless new challenges appearing on the horizon.

Appendix
MutualCity Guiding Principles

For more information about MutualCity, see the Preface.

Mutual understanding: Believing in a civic ecosystem in which a strong and healthy community benefits your organization and in which a strong and healthy organization benefits the community.

Listening: In order to understand the needs of all constituents, the organization must engage in active listening opportunities to gain understanding of the issues that influence economic revitalization, quality of life, and opportunities for all.

Connection: Connecting people and organizations that have the expertise, resources, interests, and creative problem-solving skills to take on challenges and create opportunities that lift up your community.

Action: Ensuring that key leaders and decision makers (including community representatives) are at the table to take action and that they honor the takeaways gained from engaging the community.

Collaboration: Actively and strategically working with community constituents to harness collective strengths and create greater impact.

Investing: Leveraging your resources and assets, including seeking funding from public, private, and foundation sources, to support initiatives that serve the needs of community constituents and serve the strategic plan.

Adaptiveness: Accepting the need to be flexible, to take on new challenges that provide improved strategies, and to adapt your approach when existing approaches have proven unsuccessful; this is especially crucial to ensure success in the long term.

Dreaming: Continually asking "What if?" in order to challenge your team, partners, and community constituents to imagine ideal outcomes that satisfy the previously identified needs.

Endnotes

Preface

1. Bruce Katz and Julie Wagner, "The Rise of Innovation Districts: A New Geography of Innovation in America," Metropolitan Policy Program at Brookings, May 2014, https://www.brookings.edu/essay/rise-of-innovation-districts/.

2. Not to be confused with the "anchor plus" model used by Katz and Wagner in their article to describe development around anchor institutions.

3. Isabel Schlebecker and Tonya Summerlin, "Urban Green Space: The Monon Trail, the Cultural Trail, & Gentrification," https://www.learngala.com/cases/indytrails/.

Introduction

1. Barack Obama, "Weekly Address: Making Our Communities Stronger through Fair Housing," The White House, July 11, 2015, https://obamawhitehouse.archives.gov/the-press-office/2015/07/11/weekly-address-making-our-communities-stronger-through-fair-housing.

2. Lisa Esposito, "The Countless Ways Poverty Affects People's Health," *US News*, April 20, 2016, https://health.usnews.com/health-news/patient-advice/articles/2016-04-20/the-countless-ways-poverty-affects-peoples-health.

3. Smart Growth America, "Dangerous by Design 2021," https://smartgrowthamerica.org/dangerous-by-design/.

4. Bruce Katz and Julie Wagner, "The Rise of Innovation Districts: A New

Geography of Innovation in America," Metropolitan Policy Program at Brookings, May 2014, https://www.brookings.edu/essay/rise-of-innovation-districts/.

5. Bruce Katz, "Universities," *The New Localism*, July 11, 2019, https://www.thenewlocalism.com/newsletter/universities/.

6. The real estate investment trust Ventas is a founding partner of the Global Institute on Innovation Districts (GIID); I am also a founding partner of GIID.

7. Chris David, "Austin Medical Innovation District Would Generate $800M, 2,800 New Jobs, Study Finds," KXAN, January 28, 2020, https://www.kxan.com/news/local/austin/austin-medical-innovation-district-would-generate-800m-2800-new-jobs-study-finds/.

8. "Inclusive innovation": Julie Wagner, "New Insights on How Innovation Districts Are Challenging Economic and Social Divides," The Global Institute on Innovation Districts, July 19, 2019, https://www.giid.org/how-innovation-districts-are-challenging-economic-and-social-divides/. "Common destiny": Chris Benner and Manuel Pastor, *Equity, Growth, and Community: What the Nation Can Learn from America's Metro Areas* (Oakland: University of California Press, 2015), viii.

9. Henry L. Davis, "Growing Medical Campus Steering Downtown Culture," *The Buffalo News*, January 28, 2018, https://buffalonews.com/2018/01/28/growing-medical-campus-steering-downtown-culture/.

10. Buffalo Niagara Waterkeeper, "Buffalo River Sediment Remediation," https://bnwaterkeeper.org/projects/buffalo-river-restoration/. New York State Department of Environmental Conservation, "Buffalo River Sediment Study, Buffalo(c), Erie County," March 2006, http://www.dec.ny.gov/docs/water_pdf/brsedintro.pdf.

11. Kendall Square Initiative, "Kendall Square Initiative," https://kendallsquare.mit.edu/.

12. Patrick Sisson, "As Top Innovation Hub Expands, Can Straining Local Infrastructure Keep Pace?" *Curbed*, November 6, 2018, https://www.curbed.com/2018/11/6/18067326/boston-real-estate-cambridge-mit-biotech-kendall-square.

13. Kendra R. McNeil, "Equity in Action: The Municipal Equality Index Serves as a Framework for LGBTQ+ Community Connectors," *Rapid Growth*, January 23, 2020, https://www.rapidgrowthmedia.com/features/human%20rights%20campaign_LGBTQ%20equality.aspx.

14. New York University, "Master of Urban Planning," https://wagner.nyu.edu /education/degrees/master-urban-planning/economic-development-housing.

15. "Fact Sheet: Anti-Asian Prejudice March 2020," Center for the Study of Hate & Extremism, https://www.csusb.edu/sites/default/files/FACT%20SHEET -%20Anti-Asian%20Hate%202020%203.2.21.pdf.

16. Cheryl Heller, *The Intergalactic Design Guide: Harnessing the Creative Potential of Social Design* (Washington, DC: Island Press, 2019), 45.

Chapter 1

1. Fruit Belt Community Land Trust website, https://fruitbelt-clt.org/.

2. Neighborhood Profile Data Lens, Open Data Buffalo, https://data.buffalony .gov/view/bfab-gy8p.

3. Cheryl Heller, *The Intergalactic Design Guide: Harnessing the Creative Potential of Social Design* (Washington, DC: Island Press, 2019), 216.

4. Eric Klinenberg, *Palaces for the People: How Social Infrastructure Can Help Fight Inequality, Polarization, and the Decline of Civic Life* (New York: Broadway, 2018), 9.

5. Chris Benner and Manuel Pastor, *Equity, Growth, and Community: What the Nation Can Learn from America's Metro Areas* (Oakland: University of California Press, 2015), 203.

6. Judith Rodin, *The University and Urban Revival: Out of the Ivory Tower and into the Streets* (The City in the Twenty-First Century series) (Philadelphia: University of Pennsylvania Press, 2007), 182.

7. Jacobs is also my wife's uncle, which means family dinners would have been awkward if he didn't offer support.

8. John Lewis (@repjohnlewis), Twitter, July 16, 2019, https://twitter.com /repjohnlewis/status/1151155571757867011.

9. Chris Benner, *Equity, Growth, and Community*, Kindle ed. (University of California Press, 2015).

Chapter 2

1. As I wrote in the Preface, Heller named our social design–driven approach "MutualCity." Our MutualCity guiding principles—including mutual understanding, connection, collaboration, and investing—are listed in the Appendix, along with a brief description of each principle.

2. Cheryl Heller, *The Intergalactic Design Guide: Harnessing the Creative Potential of Social Design* (Washington, DC: Island Press, 2019), 50. For much more on the topic, I highly suggest reading Heller's book, which also includes a chapter about how Heller has helped us use social design as a paid consultant for the Buffalo Niagara Medical Campus.

3. Ibid., 6.

4. *Online Etymology Dictionary*, "empathy (n.)," https://www.etymonline.com/search?q=empathy.

5. Heller, *The Intergalactic Design Guide*, 35.

6. Ryan Johnston, "San Antonio Looks to Eliminate Bias within 'Smart City' Planning," *StateScoop*, September 14, 2020, https://statescoop.com/san-antonio-eliminate-bias-smart-city-community-surveys/.

7. P. E. Moskowitz, *How to Kill a City: Gentrification, Inequality, and the Fight for the Neighborhood* (New York: Bold Type Books, 2018), 55.

8. Ibid., 67–68.

Chapter 3

1. Jane Jacobs, *The Death and Life of Great American Cities* (New York: Vintage Books, 1989), 5.

2. And yes, I recognize that name-dropping *Saturday Night Live* serves my own ego—although that's certainly not my goal.

3. Hauptman-Woodward Medical Research Institute, "Overview and History," https://hwi.buffalo.edu/about-us-old/overview/.

4. P. E. Moskowitz, *How to Kill a City: Gentrification, Inequality, and the Fight for the Neighborhood* (New York: Bold Type Books, 2018), 116.

5. Cheryl Heller, *The Intergalactic Design Guide: Harnessing the Creative Potential of Social Design* (Washington, DC: Island Press, 2019), 8.

6. David J. Hill, "Focus on Mobile Produce and Farmers Markets to Encourage Healthy Eating," *UBNow*, October 31, 2019, http://www.buffalo.edu/ubnow/stories/2019/10/mobile-farmers-markets.html.

7. Andres Duany, Elizabeth Plater-Zyberk, and Jeff Speck, *Suburban Nation: The Rise of Sprawl and the Decline of the American Dream* (New York: North Point, 2010), 36.

8. Patrick M. Condon, *Seven Rules for Sustainable Communities: Design Strategies for the Post-Carbon World* (Washington, DC: Island Press, 2010), 33.

9. Eric Klinenberg, *Palaces for the People: How Social Infrastructure Can Help Fight Inequality, Polarization, and the Decline of Civic Life* (New York: Broadway, 2018), 132–33.

10. Gabe Klein with David Vega-Barachowitz, *Start-Up City: Inspiring Private & Public Entrepreneurship, Getting Projects Done, and Having Fun* (Washington, DC: Island Press, 2015), 143.

11. Science Center, "Increasing the Depth of the Local Ecosystem," September 19, 2019, https://sciencecenter.org/news/increasing-the-depth-of-the-local -ecosystem.

12. Heller, *The Intergalactic Design Guide.*.

13. Judith Rodin, *The University and Urban Revival: Out of the Ivory Tower and into the Streets*, Kindle ed. (The City in the Twenty-First Century) (University of Pennsylvania Press, 2007), 129.

Chapter 4

1. Adam O'Daniel, "An Hour with Ed Crutchfield: Fishing, Banking and Hugh McColl," *Charlotte Business Journal*, April 18, 2013, https://www.bizjournals.com /charlotte/blog/bank_notes/2013/04/an-hour-with-ed-crutchfield-fishing.html.

2. David Hohn, speaking about Al Mugel.

3. Eric Klinenberg, *Palaces for the People: How Social Infrastructure Can Help Fight Inequality, Polarization, and the Decline of Civic Life* (New York: Broadway, 2018), 99.

4. Martha Hostetter and Sarah Klein, "Understanding and Ameliorating Medical Mistrust among Black Americans," The Commonwealth Fund, January 14, 2021, https://www.commonwealthfund.org/publications/newsletter-article /2021/jan/medical-mistrust-among-black-americans. D. P. Scharff, K. J. Mathews, P. Jackson, J. Hoffsuemmer, E. Martin, and D. Edwards, "More than Tuskegee: Understanding Mistrust about Research Participation," *Journal of Health Care for the Poor and Underserved* 21, no. 3 (2010): 879–97, doi:10.1353/hpu.0.0323.

5. Caitlin Dewey, "How Google's Bad Data Wiped a Neighborhood off the Map," *OneZero*, March 14, 2019, https://onezero.medium.com/how-googles -bad-data-wiped-a-neighborhood-off-the-map-80c4c13f1c2b.

6. Judith Rodin, *The University and Urban Revival: Out of the Ivory Tower and into the Streets* (The City in the Twenty-First Century series) (Philadelphia: University of Pennsylvania Press, 2007), 65.

7. Jim Martin, "Erie Innovation District Plots New Course," GoErie.com, February 16, 2020, https://www.goerie.com/news/20200216/erie-innovation-district -plots-new-course. Read more about the "dominant player" versus "multistake-holder" models in the article by Julie Wagner, Bruce Katz, and Thomas Osha, "The Evolution of Innovation Districts: The New Geography of Global Innovation," The Global Institute on Innovation Districts, https://www.giid.org/wp -content/uploads/2019/05/the-evolution-of-innovation-districts.pdf.

8. Hear my full podcast episode with Raja at *Talking Cities with Matt Enstice*, "Episode 18: Silicon Valley of Food Systems," February 21, 2017, http://talking cities.libsyn.com/silicon-valley-of-food-systems.

9. Grace Lazzara, "Perry Lecturer Calls for 'True Studies' of Racial Health Disparities," *UBNow*, November 25, 2020, http://www.buffalo.edu/ubnow/stories /2020/11/laveist-perry-lecture.html.

10. Transportation Electrification Partnership, LACI, "Zero Emissions 2028 Roadmap," https://roadmap.laci.org/wp-content/uploads/2019/02/LACI-ROAD MAP-V7-FINAL-HI-FI-1-020819.T6J-2.pdf.

11. G. Scott Thomas, "Business Next: Buffalo Is Now Second-Worst in the U.S. for Child Poverty," *Buffalo Business First*, September 25, 2020, https://www .bizjournals.com/buffalo/news/2020/09/25/buffalo-child-poverty-rate.html.

Evan Comen, "Detroit, Chicago, Memphis: The 25 Most Segregated Cities in America," *USA TODAY*, July 20, 2019, https://www.usatoday.com/story/money /2019/07/20/detroit-chicago-memphis-most-segregated-cities-america-housing -policy/39703787/.

Chapter 5

1. The Bridge Center for Hope, "History," https://www.brbridge.org/history.

2. Steve Hardy, "Mental Health Facility Coming to Baton Rouge after Voters Approve Tax in Landslide," *The Advocate*, December 8, 2018, https://www.the advocate.com/article_3c8dd0c4-f97b-11e8-9af9-c74d3e53e5c7.html.

3. David Freedman, "How Medellín, Colombia, Became the World's Smartest City," *Newsweek*, November 18, 2019, https://www.newsweek.com/2019/11/22/ medellin-colombia-worlds-smartest-city-1471521.html.

4. Buffalo Niagara Medical Campus, *Four Neighborhoods, One Community*, December 1, 2010, https://bnmc.org/app/uploads/2017/01/FullFourNeighbor hoods_web2.pdf.

5. Mike Keegan, "Muddy River Flood Damage Reduction and Ecosystem Restoration," U.S. Army Corps of Engineers, January 31, 2013, https://www.nae .usace.army.mil/Portals/74/docs/Topics/MuddyRiver/MuddyRiverJan2013.pdf.

6. Muddy River Restoration Project, "Emerald Necklace: Historical Photo Map," https://www.muddyrivermmoc.org/historical-photo-map/.

7. Mike Lydon and Anthony Garcia, *Tactical Urbanism: Short-Term Action for Long-Term Change* (Washington, DC: Island Press, 2015), 210.

Chapter 6

1. As Jeff Speck writes in *Walkable City Rules*, displacement "is the aspect of gentrification that most deserves our attention. . . . . While gentrification is inevitable, displacement is not." Jeff Speck, *Walkable City Rules: 101 Steps to Making Better Places* (Washington, DC: Island Press, 2018), 32.

2. Leslie Kern, *Feminist City: Claiming Space in a Man-Made World* (Brooklyn: Verso Books, 2021), 48.

3. Emily Scott, "People Are Putting Stocked Fridges on Philly Sidewalks," WHYY, August 10, 2020, https://whyy.org/articles/people-are-putting-stocked -fridges-on-philly-sidewalks/.

4. "UTA's Quest to Build Public Support," *Metro*, February 1, 2004, https:// www.metro-magazine.com/10008905/utas-quest-to-build-public-support.

5. For further discussion, see Peter Moskowitz, *How to Kill a City: Gentrification, Inequality, and the Fight for the Neighborhood* (New York: Bold Type Books, 2018), 138. And no, this is not an endorsement of Marxism, even though Karl Marx wrote about use value versus exchange value.

6. Speck, *Walkable City Rules*, 35.

7. Ibid., 10.

8. City of Spartanburg, South Carolina, "A Resolution. Healing, Reconciling, and Unity. A Pathway to a More Equitable Spartanburg," September 28, 2020, https://www.cityofspartanburg.org/cms_assets/City_Council_files/Equity .Healing.resolution.9.28.2020.pdf.

9. Madison Carter (@madisonlcarter), Twitter, October 3, 2020, https:// twitter.com/madisonlcarter/status/1319652811370541056.

10. LA Controller, "L.A. Equity Index," https://lacontroller.org/data-stories -and-maps/equityindex/.

11. Bill Lucia, "A City Looks to Incorporate More, and More Diverse, Input

into Its Budget Process," *Route Fifty*, December 2, 2020, https://www.route-fifty
.com/finance/2020/12/philadelphia-participatory-budget/170441/.

Chapter 7

1. Dan Farber, "What Steve Jobs Really Meant When He Said 'Good Artists
Copy; Great Artists Steal,'" *CNET*, January 28, 2014, https://www.cnet.com/
news/what-steve-jobs-really-meant-when-he-said-good-artists-copy-great-artists
-steal/.

2. Mary Mack, "Conceiving CORTEX (Early Years 2000–2002): Building
a New Innovation District in St. Louis," *Entrepreneur Quarterly* (EQ), April
20, 2020, https://eqstl.com/conceiving-cortex-cortex-special-feature-chapter-1
-2000-2002/.

3. Greater Phoenix Chamber of Commerce, "Buffalo Niagara Medical Campus: Benchmarking 2017, June 18–20 2017," https://www.phoenixchamber.com
/wp-content/uploads/2017/10/June-2017-Buffalo-Benchmarking-Recap.pdf.

4. Greater Cleveland Regional Transit Authority, "RTA's HealthLine: The
World-Class Standard for BRT Service," http://www.riderta.com/healthline/
about.

5. Chris Benner and Manuel Pastor, *Equity, Growth, and Community: What
the Nation Can Learn from America's Metro Areas* (Oakland: University of California Press, 2015), 185.

6. Yogi Berra, *You Can Observe a Lot by Watching: What I've Learned about
Teamwork from the Yankees and Life* (Hoboken, NJ: Wiley, 2009).

7. Jane Jacobs, *The Death and Life of Great American Cities* (New York: Vintage
Books, 1989), 442.

8. Eric Klinenberg, *Palaces for the People: How Social Infrastructure Can Help
Fight Inequality, Polarization, and the Decline of Civic Life* (New York: Broadway,
2018), 4.

9. Patrick M. Condon, *Seven Rules for Sustainable Communities: Design Strategies for the Post-Carbon World* (Washington, DC: Island Press, 2010), 68, citing Donald Watson, Alan Plattus, and Robert Shibley, *Time-Saver Standards for
Urban Design* (New York: McGraw-Hill, 2003).

10. Jeff Speck, *Walkable City: How Downtown Can Save America, One Step at
a Time* (New York: North Point Press, 2012), 174, citing Andres Duany, Elizabeth Plater-Zyberk, and Jeff Speck, *Suburban Nation: The Rise of Sprawl and the
Decline of the American Dream* (New York: North Point Press, 2000), 36–37.

11. Ibid., 174..

12. Gabe Klein with David Vega-Barachowitz, *Start-Up City: Inspiring Private & Public Entrepreneurship, Getting Projects Done, and Having Fun* (Washington, DC: Island Press, 2015), 107.

13. Christele Harrouk, "UN-Habitat Promotes Inclusive Planning and Gender Equitable Cities Using Technology," *ArchDaily*, January 2, 2020, https://www.archdaily.com/931217/un-habitat-promotes-inclusive-planning-and-gender-equitable-cities-using-technology.

14. For another great lesson on studying failure, read about how Abraham Wald determined the optimal placement for aircraft armor in World War II by thinking about the planes that didn't make it back from their missions. You'll find a writeup in Jordan Ellenberg's *How Not to Be Wrong: The Power of Mathematical Thinking* (New York: London: Penguin Books, 2015).

15. College for Creative Studies, "Which Way Forward? Equitable Mobility for Detroit in 2030," December 1, 2020, https://www.collegeforcreativestudies.edu/articles/mfa-integrated-design-project-on-display.

16. Mike Lydon and Anthony Garcia, *Tactical Urbanism: Short-Term Action for Long-Term Change* (Washington, DC: Island Press, 2015), 180.

Chapter 8

1. Larry Jacobs was also my father-in-law, which means I had the honor of seeing his extraordinary vision firsthand. The Jacobs family has honored Larry's commitment to improving healthcare by contributing more than $50 million to health-related organizations, including gifts to establish the Jacobs Institute and support the University at Buffalo's Jacobs School of Medicine and Biomedical Sciences, both of which are located on the Buffalo Niagara Medical Campus.

2. Henry L. Davis, "Growing Medical Campus Steering Downtown Culture," *The Buffalo News*, January 28, 2018, https://buffalonews.com/2018/01/28/growing-medical-campus-steering-downtown-culture/.

3. Community Solutions, "The MacArthur Foundation Awards Community Solutions $100 Million to Accelerate an End to Homelessness in the U.S.," April 7, 2021, https://community.solutions/the-macarthur-foundation-awards-community-solutions-100-million-to-accelerate-an-end-to-homelessness-in-the-u-s/.

4. Erie County, New York, Department of Health, "Erie County, New York, Community Health Assessment 2019–2022," http://www2.erie.gov/health/sites/www2.erie.gov.health/files/uploads/pdfs/CHA.pdf.

5. Next City, "Next City's 19 Best Solutions of 2019," December 30, 2019, https://nextcity.org/features/view/next-citys-19-best-solutions-of-2019.

6. Jeff Speck, *Walkable City: How Downtown Can Save America, One Step at a Time* (New York: North Point Press, 2012), 238.

7. Laura Bliss, "Las Vegas Gambles on a 'Smart City' Technology Makeover," *Bloomberg CityLab*, February 27, 2019, https://www.citylab.com/solutions/2019/02/las-vegas-smart-city-technology-surveillance-data-privacy/583474/.

Chapter 9

1. Mike Lydon and Anthony Garcia, *Tactical Urbanism: Short-Term Action for Long-Term Change* (Washington, DC: Island Press, 2015), 2.

2. Ibid., 110.

3. Ibid., 110.

4. "Sewing Hope in the Lives of Others," *Talking Cities with Matt Enstice* podcast, June 13, 2017, https://talkingcities.libsyn.com/sewing-hope-in-the-lives-of-others.

5. Ryan McGreal, "City Crackdown on Tactical Urbanism," *Raise the Hammer*, May 9, 2013, https://raisethehammer.org/article/1850/.

6. Emily Nonko, "How the Oregon Convention Center Put Equity First," *Next City*, September 24, 2020, https://nextcity.org/daily/entry/how-the-oregon-convention-center-put-equity-first.

Chapter 10

1. If you want to be formal about it, you can talk about bridges in terms of "social capital" and "social infrastructure," as Eric Klinenberg wrote about in *Palaces for the People: How Social Infrastructure Can Help Fight Inequality, Polarization, and the Decline of Civic Life* (New York: Broadway, 2018), 5. Social capital measures the connections between people; social infrastructure includes the physical environment and organizations that shape their relationships. Well-designed social infrastructure—from parks and libraries to neighborhood groups and houses of worship—can help build social capital and strengthen communities.

2. Rob Fairlie, "Financing Black-Owned Businesses," Stanford Institute for Economic Policy Research, May 2017, https://siepr.stanford.edu/publications/policy-brief/financing-black-owned-businesses.

3. Anthony Schoettle, "Cultural Trail Becomes Unique Drawing Card for Conventions and Trade Shows," *Indianapolis Business Journal*, November 2, 2017,

https://www.ibj.com/articles/66105-cultural-trail-becomes-unique-drawing
-card-for-conventions-and-trade-shows.

4. Lisa Yazel-Smith, Andrew Merkley, Robin Danek, and Cynthia L. Stone, "Expanding the Indianapolis Cultural Trail: A Health Impact Assessment," *Chronicles of Health Impact Assessment* 3, no. 1 (2018). This report also contains discussions about the art that appears along the trail, including opportunities for "local art, specifically art relative to the African American community who first settled the area and continue to inhabit it."

5. Carlos Mejia, "A History of Racial Disparity in American Public Swimming Pools," Connecticut Public Radio, June 6, 2018, https://www.wnpr.org/post/ history-racial-disparity-american-public-swimming-pools.

6. Evelyn Nieves, "In the Wake of a Teen-Ager's Death, a Cloud of Racism, Then a Lawsuit," *New York Times*, December 19, 1996, https://www.nytimes .com/1996/12/19/nyregion/in-the-wake-of-a-teen-ager-s-death-a-cloud-of -racism-then-a-lawsuit.html.

Chapter 11

1. Pam is my mother-in-law, and I'm extraordinarily proud of her work.

2. P. E. Moskowitz, *How to Kill a City: Gentrification, Inequality, and the Fight for the Neighborhood* (New York: Bold Type Books, 2018), 206.

3. Buffalo Niagara Medical Campus, "Highlighting BNMC Spark 2019 Projects," November 27, 2019, video, 1:09, https://bnmc.org/bnmc-spark-2019 -project-highlights/.

Chapter 12

1. Neil Smith, "Toward a Theory of Gentrification A Back to the City Movement by Capital, Not People," *Journal of the American Planning Association* 45, no. 4 (1979): 538–48, doi:10.1080/01944367908977002.

2. Ellen Goldbaum, "UB–Community Partnership Helping to Blunt Effect of Pandemic on Buffalo's Most Vulnerable Citizens," *UBNow*, October 14, 2020, http://www.buffalo.edu/ubnow/stories/2020/10/cheri-update.html.

3. Patrick Sisson, "As Sea Level Rises, Miami Neighborhoods Feel Rising Tide of Gentrification," *Curbed*, February 10, 2020, https://www.curbed.com/2020/2 /10/21128496/miami-real-estate-climate-change-gentrification.

4. Bob Ross, *Happy Little Accidents: The Wit & Wisdom of Bob Ross* (New York: Running Press, 2017).

5. Public Art Saint Paul, "Sidewalk Poetry," http://publicartstpaul.org/project/poetry/#about_the_project.

6. Kate Elizabeth Queram, "How One City Went Virtual in 30 Days," *Route Fifty Today*, July 17, 2020, https://www.route-fifty.com/tech-data/2020/07/how-one-city-went-virtual-30-days/166958/.

7. Felicia Henry and Scott Gabriel Knowles, "3 Big Ideas to Fuel an Equitable COVID Recovery," *WHYY*, October 22, 2020, https://whyy.org/articles/3-big-ideas-to-fuel-an-equitable-covid-recovery/. Reprinted with the permission of WHYY, Inc.

Conclusion

1. Dennis Elsenbeck, former New York State regional director, National Grid. Edison didn't actually touch the lines in our system, but he did visit predecessors to our current utilities, and you can find his signature on some of their documents.

2. Forest Service, U.S. Department of Agriculture, Eastern Region R9 Regional Office, "International Day of Forests," https://www.fs.usda.gov/detail/r9/home/?cid=stelprd3832558.

3. U.S. Census Bureau, "Projecting Majority-Minority," https://www.census.gov/content/dam/Census/newsroom/releases/2015/cb15-tps16_graphic.pdf.

4. Like many of our peer innovation districts, we're working to diversify our own organization and promote diversity in our member anchor institutions.

5. New American Economy, "Immigrants and the Growth of America's Largest Cities," July 10, 2019, https://research.newamericaneconomy.org/report/immigrants-and-the-growth-of-americas-largest-cities/.

6. Kim Parker, Nikki Graf, and Ruth Igielnik, "Generation Z Looks a Lot Like Millennials on Key Social and Political Issues," Pew Research Center, January 17, 2019, https://www.pewresearch.org/social-trends/2019/01/17/generation-z-looks-a-lot-like-millennials-on-key-social-and-political-issues/.

7. Jillian Du and Anjali Mahendra, "Too Many Cities Are Growing Out Rather than Up. 3 Reasons That's a Problem," World Resources Institute, January 31, 2019, https://www.wri.org/blog/2019/01/too-many-cities-are-growing-out-rather-3-reasons-s-problem.

8. ICMA, "A New Kind of CEO: The Role of the Chief Equity Officer (and Other Equity Positions)," October 1, 2020, https://icma.org/articles/pm-magazine/new-kind-ceo-role-chief-equity-officer-and-other-equity-positions.

9. "Meet the Chief Equity Officers," Bloomberg Cities Network, May 5, 2021, https://bloombergcities.jhu.edu/news/meet-chief-equity-officers.

10. Julie Wagner, "How Cleveland's Innovation District Is Advancing Equity through a New Kind of Anchor Institution," *Brookings*, November 9, 2020, https://www.brookings.edu/blog/the-avenue/2020/11/09/how-clevelands-innovation-district-is-advancing-equity-through-a-new-kind-of-anchor-institution/.

11. Bureau of Labor Statistics, "Employment Projections—2019–2029," September 1, 2020, https://www.bls.gov/news.release/pdf/ecopro.pdf. The two lowest-paying jobs are personal care aide and home health aide.

12. Chris Caulfield, "The Gig Economy Has Arrived in the World of Nursing," Forbes Technology Council, September 27, 2019, https://www.forbes.com/sites/forbestechcouncil/2019/09/27/the-gig-economy-has-arrived-in-the-world-of-nursing/.

13. K. K. Y. Liu and B. A. Baskaran, "Thermal Performance of Extensive Green Roofs in Cold Climates," NRC Publications Archive, 2005 World Sustainable Building Conference [Proceedings], pp. 1–8, September 1, 2005, https://nrc-publications.canada.ca/eng/view/accepted/?id=11095d5f-ac30-41f3-9340-2f2382ba40de.

14. Zainab Baloch, "2040 Vision: What Will the Triangle's Social Justice Movements Look Like in 2040?" *INDY Week*, December 31, 2019, https://indyweek.com/news/northcarolina/2040-vision-social-justice/.

15. David J. Hill, "UB Researchers, Students Are Shaping Important Conversations around Equity in Food Systems," University at Buffalo News Center, October 12, 2017, http://www.buffalo.edu/news/releases/2017/10/022.html.

16. Jason Plautz, "LA Wants to Reach 30% EVs on Roads by 2028 Olympics," *Smart Cities Dive*, December 3, 2019, https://www.smartcitiesdive.com/news/la-wants-to-reach-30-evs-on-roads-by-2028-olympics/568305/.

17. Office of Energy Efficiency & Renewable Energy, U.S. Department of Energy, "Low-Income Community Energy Solutions," https://www.energy.gov/eere/slsc/low-income-community-energy-solutions.

18. D. A. Sunter, S. Castellanos, and D. M. Kammen, "Disparities in Rooftop Photovoltaics Deployment in the United States by Race and Ethnicity," *Nature Sustainability* 2 (2019): 71–76, https://doi.org/10.1038/s41893-018-0204-z.

19. I've served on the advisory board for Viridi Parente and currently serve on their board of directors.

20. Gabe Klein with David Vega-Barachowitz, *Start-Up City: Inspiring Private*

& Public Entrepreneurship, Getting Projects Done, and Having Fun (Washington, DC: Island Press, 2015), 197.

21. Ibid., 199.

22. Ellen Barry, "Should Public Transit Be Free? More Cities Say, Why Not?" *New York Times*, January 14, 2020, https://www.nytimes.com/2020/01/14/us/free-public-transit.html.

23. Remington Tonar and Ellis Talton, "Cities Need to Rethink Micromobility to Ensure It Works for All," *Forbes*, January 7, 2020, https://www.forbes.com/sites/ellistalton/2020/01/07/cities-need-to-rethink-micromobility-to-ensure-it-works-for-all/.

24. U.S. Government Accountability Office, "Investment Management: Key Practices Could Provide More Options for Federal Entities and Opportunities for Minority- and Women-Owned Asset Managers," GAO-17-726, September 13, 2017, https://www.gao.gov/products/GAO-17-726.

25. Oscar Perry Abello, "To St. Louis Municipal Bank Accounts, Black Lives Matter," *Next City*, May 14, 2019, https://nextcity.org/daily/entry/to-st-louis-municipal-bank-accounts-black-lives-matter. Also see "Next City's 19 Best Solutions of 2019," *Next City*, December 30, 2019, https://nextcity.org/features/view/next-citys-19-best-solutions-of-2019.

26. Fruit Belt Community Land Trust website, accessed September 12, 2021, https://fruitbelt-clt.org/.

27. Butler was an African-American science fiction writer who earned a MacArthur Fellowship along with multiple literary awards; she grew up watching her mother going in through the back doors of houses to clean them.

References and Readings

Abello, Oscar Perry. "The Making of an Equitable Community Development Loan Product." *Next City*, December 31, 2019. https://nextcity.org/daily/entry/the-making-of-an-equitable-community-development-loan-product.

Abello, Oscar Perry. "To St. Louis Municipal Bank Accounts, Black Lives Matter." *Next City*, May 14, 2019. https://nextcity.org/daily/entry/to-st-louis-municipal-bank-accounts-black-lives-matter.

Anchor District Council. https://anchordistrictcouncil.org/.

Association of University Research Parks. https://www.aurp.net/.

Baloch, Zainab. "2040 Vision: What Will the Triangle's Social Justice Movements Look Like in 2040?" *INDY Week*, December 31, 2019. https://indyweek.com/news/northcarolina/2040-vision-social-justice/.

Barry, Ellen. "Should Public Transit Be Free? More Cities Say, Why Not?" *New York Times*, January 14, 2020. https://www.nytimes.com/2020/01/14/us/free-public-transit.html.

Benner, Chris, and Manuel Pastor. *Equity, Growth, and Community: What the Nation Can Learn from America's Metro Areas.* Oakland: University of California Press, 2015.

Berra, Yogi. *You Can Observe a Lot by Watching: What I've Learned about Teamwork from the Yankees and Life.* Hoboken, NJ: Wiley, 2009.

Blatto, Anna. "A City Divided: A Brief History of Segregation in Buffalo." Partnership for the Public Good and OpenBuffalo, April 2018.

Bliss, Laura. "Las Vegas Gambles on a 'Smart City' Technology Makeover." *Bloomberg CityLab*, February 27, 2019. https://www.citylab.com/solutions/2019/02/las-vegas-smart-city-technology-surveillance-data-privacy/583474/.

Bloomberg Cities Network. "Meet the Chief Equity Officers." May 5, 2021. https://bloombergcities.jhu.edu/news/meet-chief-equity-officers.

Bowdler, Janis, Henry Cisneros, and Jeffrey Lubell. *Building Equitable Cities: How to Drive Economic Mobility and Regional Growth.* Washington, DC: Urban Land Institute, 2017.

The Bridge Center for Hope. "History." https://www.brbridge.org/history.

Buffalo Niagara Medical Campus. "Four Neighborhoods, One Community." December 1, 2010. https://bnmc.org/app/uploads/2017/01/FullFourNeighborhoods_web2.pdf.

Buffalo Niagara Medical Campus. "Highlighting BNMC Spark 2019 Projects." November 27, 2019, video, 1:09. https://bnmc.org/bnmc-spark-2019-project-highlights/.

Buffalo Niagara Waterkeeper. "Buffalo River Sediment Remediation." https://bnwaterkeeper.org/projects/buffalo-river-restoration/.

Bureau of Labor Statistics. "Employment Projections—2019–2029." September 1, 2020. https://www.bls.gov/news.release/pdf/ecopro.pdf.

Carter, Madison (@madisonlcarter). Twitter, October 3, 2020. https://twitter.com/madisonlcarter/status/1319652811370541056.

Caulfield, Chris. "The Gig Economy Has Arrived in the World of Nursing." Forbes Technology Council, September 27, 2019. https://www.forbes.com/sites/forbestechcouncil/2019/09/27/the-gig-economy-has-arrived-in-the-world-of-nursing/.

Cities for Our Time: Fall 2014 Competition Entries. Berkeley: Alfred Twu, 2014. https://www.amazon.com/gp/product/1503067076/.

City of Spartanburg, South Carolina. "A Resolution. Healing, Reconciling, and Unity. A Pathway to a More Equitable Spartanburg." September 28, 2020. https://www.cityofspartanburg.org/cms_assets/City_Council_files/Equity.Healing.resolution.9.28.2020.pdf.

College for Creative Studies. "Which Way Forward? Equitable Mobility for Detroit in 2030." December 1, 2020. https://www.collegeforcreativestudies.edu/articles/mfa-integrated-design-project-on-display.

Comen, Evan. "Detroit, Chicago, Memphis: The 25 most segregated cities in

America." *USA Today*, July 20, 2019. https://www.usatoday.com/story/money/2019/07/20/detroit-chicago-memphis-most-segregated-cities-america-housing-policy/39703787/.

Community Solutions. "The MacArthur Foundation Awards Community Solutions $100 Million to Accelerate an End to Homelessness in the U.S." April 7, 2021. https://community.solutions/the-macarthur-foundation-awards-community-solutions-100-million-to-accelerate-an-end-to-homelessness-in-the-u-s/.

Condon, Patrick M. *Seven Rules for Sustainable Communities: Design Strategies for the Post-Carbon World*. Washington, DC: Island Press, 2010.

Crowe, Cailin. "Las Vegas Targets SF, Seattle Remote Workers in Relocation Campaign." *Smart Cities Dive*, November 16, 2020. https://www.smartcitiesdive.com/news/las-vegas-targets-sf-seattle-remote-workers-in-relocation-campaign/589068/.

David, Chris. "Austin Medical Innovation District Would Generate $800M, 2,800 New Jobs, Study Finds." *KXAN*. January 28, 2020. https://www.kxan.com/news/local/austin/austin-medical-innovation-district-would-generate-800m-2800-new-jobs-study-finds/.

Davis, Henry L. "Growing Medical Campus Steering Downtown Culture." *The Buffalo News*, January 28, 2018. https://buffalonews.com/2018/01/28/growing-medical-campus-steering-downtown-culture/.

Dewey, Caitlin. "How Google's Bad Data Wiped a Neighborhood off the Map." *OneZero*, March 14, 2019. https://onezero.medium.com/how-googles-bad-data-wiped-a-neighborhood-off-the-map-80c4c13f1c2b.

Du, Jillian, and Anjali Mahendra. "Too Many Cities Are Growing Out Rather than Up. 3 Reasons That's a Problem." World Resources Institute. January 31, 2019. https://www.wri.org/blog/2019/01/too-many-cities-are-growing-out-rather-3-reasons-s-problem.

Duany, Andres, Elizabeth Plater-Zyberk, and Jeff Speck. *Suburban Nation: The Rise of Sprawl and the Decline of the American Dream*. New York: North Point, 2010.

Ellenberg, Jordan. *How Not to Be Wrong: The Power of Mathematical Thinking*. New York: Penguin Books, 2015.

Erie County, New York, Department of Health. "Erie County, New York, Community Health Assessment 2019–2022." http://www2.erie.gov/health/sites/www2.erie.gov.health/files/uploads/pdfs/CHA.pdf.

Esposito, Lisa. "The Countless Ways Poverty Affects People's Health." *US News*, April 20, 2016. https://health.usnews.com/health-news/patient-advice/articles /2016-04-20/the-countless-ways-poverty-affects-peoples-health.

"Fact Sheet: Anti-Asian Prejudice March 2020." Center for the Study of Hate & Extremism. https://www.csusb.edu/sites/default/files/FACT%20SHEET-%20 Anti-Asian%20Hate%202020%203.2.21.pdf.

Fairbanks, Phil. "Feds Arrest Buffalo's 'Biggest Drug Trafficker'." *The Buffalo News*, February 21, 2020. https://buffalonews.com/2020/02/21/feds-arrest-buffalos -biggest-drug-trafficker/.

Fairlie, Rob. "Financing Black-Owned Businesses." Stanford Institute for Economic Policy Research, May 2017. https://siepr.stanford.edu/research/publications /financing-black-owned-businesses.

Farber, Dan. "What Steve Jobs Really Meant When He Said 'Good Artists Copy; Great Artists Steal'." *CNET*, January 28, 2014. https://www.cnet.com/news/what -steve-jobs-really-meant-when-he-said-good-artists-copy-great-artists-steal/.

Forest Service, U.S. Department of Agriculture, Eastern Region R9 Regional Office. "International Day of Forests." https://www.fs.usda.gov/detail/r9/ home/?cid=stelprd3832558.

Freedman, David. "How Medellín, Colombia, Became the World's Smartest City." *Newsweek*, November 18, 2019. https://www.newsweek.com/2019/11 /22/medellin-colombia-worlds-smartest-city-1471521.html.

Fruit Belt Community Land Trust. https://fruitbelt-clt.org/.

The Global Institute on Innovation Districts. https://www.giid.org/.

Goldbaum, Ellen. "UB–Community Partnership Helping to Blunt Effect of Pandemic on Buffalo's Most Vulnerable Citizens." *UBNow*, October 14, 2020. http: //www.buffalo.edu/ubnow/stories/2020/10/cheri-update.html.

Greater Cleveland Regional Transit Authority. "RTA's HealthLine—The World -Class Standard for BRT Service." http://www.riderta.com/healthline/about.

Greater Phoenix Chamber of Commerce. "Buffalo Niagara Medical Campus: Benchmarking 2017, June 18–20 2017." https://www.phoenixchamber.com /wp-content/uploads/2017/10/June-2017-Buffalo-Benchmarking-Recap.pdf.

Hardy, Steve. "Mental Health Facility Coming to Baton Rouge after Voters Approve Tax in Landslide." *The Advocate*, December 8, 2018. https://www .theadvocate.com/article_3c8dd0c4-f97b-11e8-9af9-c74d3e53e5c7.html.

Harrouk, Christele. "UN-Habitat Promotes Inclusive Planning and Gender Equitable Cities Using Technology." *ArchDaily*, January 2, 2020. https://www .archdaily.com/931217/un-habitat-promotes-inclusive-planning-and-gender -equitable-cities-using-technology.

Hauck, Grace. "Emmett Till's Lynching Ignited a Civil Rights Movement. Historians Say George Floyd's Death Could Do the Same." *USA Today*, June 6, 2020. https://www.usatoday.com/story/news/nation/2020/06/06/george-floyd -emmett-till-deaths-inspire-calls-change-justice/3135768001/.

Hauptman-Woodward Medical Research Institute. "Overview and History." https://hwi.buffalo.edu/about-us-old/overview/.

Heller, Cheryl. *The Intergalactic Design Guide: Harnessing the Creative Potential of Social Design*. Washington, DC: Island Press, 2019.

Henry, Felicia, and Scott Gabriel Knowles. "3 Big Ideas to Fuel an Equitable COVID Recovery." *WHYY*, October 22, 2020. https://whyy.org/articles/3 -big-ideas-to-fuel-an-equitable-covid-recovery/.

Hill, David J. "Focus on Mobile Produce and Farmers Markets to Encourage Healthy Eating." *UBNow*, October 31, 2019. http://www.buffalo.edu/ubnow /stories/2019/10/mobile-farmers-markets.html.

Hill, David J. "UB Researchers, Students Are Shaping Important Conversations around Equity in Food Systems." University at Buffalo News Center, October 12, 2017. http://www.buffalo.edu/news/releases/2017/10/022.html.

Hostetter, Martha, and Sarah Klein. "Understanding and Ameliorating Medical Mistrust among Black Americans." The Commonwealth Fund, January 14, 2021. https://www.commonwealthfund.org/publications/newsletter-article/2021 /jan/medical-mistrust-among-black-americans.

ICMA. "A New Kind of CEO: The Role of the Chief Equity Officer (and Other Equity Positions)." October 1, 2020. https://icma.org/articles/pm-magazine/ new-kind-ceo-role-chief-equity-officer-and-other-equity-positions.

International Business Innovation Association. https://inbia.org/.

Jacobs, Jane. *The Death and Life of Great American Cities*. New York: Vintage Books, 1989.

Johnston, Ryan. "San Antonio Looks to Eliminate Bias within 'Smart City' Planning." *StateScoop*, September 14, 2020. https://statescoop.com/san-antonio -eliminate-bias-smart-city-community-surveys/.

Katz, Bruce. "Universities." *The New Localism*, July 11, 2019. https://www.thenew localism.com/newsletter/universities/.

Katz, Bruce, and Julie Wagner. "The Rise of Innovation Districts: A New Geography of Innovation in America." Metropolitan Policy Program at Brookings, May 2014. https://www.brookings.edu/essay/rise-of-innovation-districts/.

Keegan, Mike. "Muddy River Flood Damage Reduction and Ecosystem Restoration." United States Army Corps of Engineers, January 31, 2013. https://www.nae.usace.army.mil/Portals/74/docs/Topics/MuddyRiver/MuddyRiver Jan2013.pdf.

Kendall Square Initiative. "Kendall Square Initiative." https://kendallsquare.mit .edu/.

Kern, Leslie. *Feminist City: Claiming Space in a Man-Made World*. Brooklyn: Verso Books, 2021.

Klein, Gabe, with David Vega-Barachowitz. *Start-Up City: Inspiring Private & Public Entrepreneurship, Getting Projects Done, and Having Fun*. Washington, DC: Island Press, 2015.

Klinenberg, Eric. *Palaces For the People: How Social Infrastructure Can Help Fight Inequality, Polarization, and the Decline of Civic Life*. New York: Broadway, 2018.

Koran, Mario. "California Just Legalized Public Banking, Setting the Stage for More Affordable Housing." *The Guardian*, October 4, 2019. https://www.the guardian.com/us-news/2019/oct/03/california-governor-public-banking-law -ab857.

LA Controller. "L.A. Equity Index." https://lacontroller.org/data-stories-and -maps/equityindex/.

Lantero, Allison. "The War of the Currents: AC vs. DC Power." Department of Energy, November 18, 2014. https://www.energy.gov/articles/war-currents-ac -vs-dc-power.

Lazzara, Grace. "Perry Lecturer Calls for 'True Studies' of Racial Health Disparities." *UBNow*, November 25, 2020. http://www.buffalo.edu/ubnow/stories /2020/11/laveist-perry-lecture.html.

Lewis, John (@repjohnlewis). Twitter, July 16, 2019. https://twitter.com/repjohn lewis/status/1151155571757867011.

Liu, K. K. Y., and B. A. Baskaran. "Thermal Performance of Extensive Green Roofs in Cold Climates." NRC Publications Archive. 2005 World Sustainable Building Conference [Proceedings], pp. 1–8, September 1, 2005. https://nrc

-publications.canada.ca/eng/view/accepted/?id=11095d5f-ac30-41f3-9340
-2f2382ba40de.

Lucia, Bill. "A City Looks to Incorporate More, and More Diverse, Input into Its
Budget Process." *Route Fifty*, December 2, 2020. https://www.route-fifty.com
/finance/2020/12/philadelphia-participatory-budget/170441/.

Lydon, Mike, and Anthony Garcia. *Tactical Urbanism: Short-Term Action for
Long-Term Change*. Washington, DC: Island Press, 2015.

Mack, Mary. "Conceiving CORTEX (Early Years 2000–2002): Building a New
Innovation District in St. Louis." *Entrepreneur Quarterly (EQ)*, April 20, 2020.
https://eqstl.com/conceiving-cortex-cortex-special-feature-chapter-1-2000
-2002/.

Martin, Jim. "Erie Innovation District Plots New Course." GoErie.com, February 16,
2020. https://www.goerie.com/news/20200216/erie-innovation-district-plots
-new-course.

McGreal, Ryan. "City Crackdown on Tactical Urbanism." *Raise the Hammer*,
May 9, 2013. https://raisethehammer.org/article/1850/.

McNeil, Kendra R. "Equity in Action: The Municipal Equality Index Serves as
a Framework for LGBTQ+ Community Connectors." *Rapid Growth*, January 23, 2020. https://www.rapidgrowthmedia.com/features/human%20rights
%20campaign_LGBTQ%20equality.aspx.

Mejia, Carlos. "A History of Racial Disparity in American Public Swimming
Pools." Connecticut Public Radio, June 6, 2018. https://www.wnpr.org/post/
history-racial-disparity-american-public-swimming-pools.

Metro. "UTA's Quest to Build Public Support." February 1, 2004. https://www
.metro-magazine.com/10008905/utas-quest-to-build-public-support.

Morrison, Arnault. *Innovation Districts: A Toolkit for Urban Leaders*. 2015. https:
//www.amazon.com/gp/product/B012FL8GJI/?asin=B012FL8GJI&revision
Id=&format=2&depth=1.

Moskowitz, P. E. *How to Kill a City: Gentrification, Inequality, and the Fight for the
Neighborhood*. New York: Bold Type Books, 2018.

Muddy River Restoration Project. "Emerald Necklace: Historical Photo Map."
https://www.muddyrivermmoc.org/historical-photo-map/.

National Grid. "Implementation Plan for Fruit Belt Neighborhood Solar REV
Demonstration in Buffalo, New York." January 4, 2016. http://documents.
dps.ny.gov/public/Common/ViewDoc.aspx?DocRefId=%7BAFABE824
-60F5-4800-9D28-5FC1A69B4D83%7D.

National League of Cities. https://www.nlc.org/.

Neighborhood Profile Data Lens. *Open Data Buffalo*. https://data.buffalony.gov /view/bfab-gy8p.

New American Economy. "Immigrants and the Growth of America's Largest Cities." July 10, 2019. https://research.newamericaneconomy.org/report/immi grants-and-the-growth-of-americas-largest-cities/.

New York State Department of Environmental Conservation. "Buffalo River Sediment Study, Buffalo(c), Erie County." March 2006. http://www.dec.ny .gov/docs/water_pdf/brsedintro.pdf.

New York University. "Master of Urban Planning." https://wagner.nyu.edu/edu cation/degrees/master-urban-planning/economic-development-housing.

Newman, Peter, Timothy Beatley, and Heather Boyer. *Resilient Cities: Overcoming Fossil Fuel Dependence*. 2nd ed. Washington, DC: Island Press, 2017.

Next City. "Next City's 19 Best Solutions of 2019." December 30, 2019. https:// nextcity.org/features/view/next-citys-19-best-solutions-of-2019.

Nieves, Evelyn. "In the Wake of a Teen-Ager's Death, a Cloud of Racism, Then a Lawsuit." *New York Times*, December 19, 1996. https://www.nytimes.com /1996/12/19/nyregion/in-the-wake-of-a-teen-ager-s-death-a-cloud-of-racism -then-a-lawsuit.html.

Nonko, Emily. "How the Oregon Convention Center Put Equity First." *Next City*, September 24, 2020, https://nextcity.org/daily/entry/how-the-oregon -convention-center-put-equity-first.

Obama, Barack. "Weekly Address: Making Our Communities Stronger through Fair Housing." The White House, July 11, 2015. https://obamawhitehouse .archives.gov/the-press-office/2015/07/11/weekly-address-making-our-com munities-stronger-through-fair-housing.

O'Daniel, Adam. "An Hour with Ed Crutchfield: Fishing, Banking and Hugh McColl." *Charlotte Business Journal*, April 18, 2013. https://www.bizjournals .com/charlotte/blog/bank_notes/2013/04/an-hour-with-ed-crutchfield-fish ing.html.

Office of Energy Efficiency & Renewable Energy, U.S. Department of Energy. "Low-Income Community Energy Solutions." https://www.energy.gov/eere/ slsc/low-income-community-energy-solutions.

Online Etymology Dictionary. "empathy (n.)." https://www.etymonline.com/ search?q=empathy.

Parker, Kim, Nikki Graf, and Ruth Igielnik. "Generation Z Looks a Lot Like Millennials on Key Social and Political Issues." Pew Research Center, January 17, 2019. https://www.pewresearch.org/social-trends/2019/01/17/generation -z-looks-a-lot-like-millennials-on-key-social-and-political-issues/.

Plautz, Jason. "LA Wants to Reach 30% EVs on Roads by 2028 Olympics." *Smart Cities Dive*, December 3, 2019. https://www.smartcitiesdive.com/news /la-wants-to-reach-30-evs-on-roads-by-2028-olympics/568305/.

Public Art Saint Paul. "Sidewalk Poetry." http://publicartstpaul.org/project/ poetry/#about_the_project.

Queram, Kate Elizabeth. "How One City Went Virtual in 30 Days." *Route Fifty Today*, July 17, 2020. https://www.route-fifty.com/tech-data/2020/07/how -one-city-went-virtual-30-days/166958/.

Rey, Jay. "Coalition Renews Push for November School Board Elections in Buffalo." *The Buffalo News*, June 1, 2018. https://buffalonews.com/news/local /coalition-renews-push-for-november-school-board-elections-in-buffalo/ article_a2112a4f-f1fe-56aa-974f-cde9e8d46e73.html.

Rodin, Judith. *The University and Urban Revival: Out of the Ivory Tower and into the Streets* (The City in the Twenty-First Century series). Philadelphia: University of Pennsylvania Press, 2007.

Ross, Bob. *Happy Little Accidents: The Wit & Wisdom of Bob Ross*. New York: Running Press, 2017.

Scharff, D. P., K. J. Mathews, P. Jackson, J. Hoffsuemmer, E. Martin, and D. Edwards. "More than Tuskegee: Understanding Mistrust about Research Participation." *Journal of Health Care for the Poor and Underserved*. 21, no. 3 (2010): 879–97. doi:10.1353/hpu.0.0323.

Schlebecker, Isabel, and Tonya Summerlin. "Urban Green Space: The Monon Trail, the Cultural Trail, & Gentrification." https://www.learngala.com/cases /indytrails/.

Schoettle, Anthony. "Cultural Trail Becomes Unique Drawing Card for Conventions and Trade Shows." *Indianapolis Business Journal*, November 2, 2017. https://www.ibj.com/articles/66105-cultural-trail-becomes-unique-drawing -card-for-conventions-and-trade-shows.

Science Center. "Increasing the Depth of the Local Ecosystem." September 19, 2019. https://sciencecenter.org/news/increasing-the-depth-of-the-local-ecosystem.

Scott, Emily. "People Are Putting Stocked Fridges on Philly Sidewalks." *WHYY*,

August 10, 2020. https://whyy.org/articles/people-are-putting-stocked-fridges
-on-philly-sidewalks/.

Seavers, Dean. "The Democratization of Energy." *National Grid*, January 2017.
https://www.nationalgridus.com/media/pdfs/our-company/ng_ebook.pdf.

Sisson, Patrick. "As Sea Level Rises, Miami Neighborhoods Feel Rising Tide of
Gentrification." *Curbed*, February 10, 2020. https://www.curbed.com/2020
/2/10/21128496/miami-real-estate-climate-change-gentrification.

Sisson, Patrick. "As Top Innovation Hub Expands, Can Straining Local Infrastructure Keep Pace?" *Curbed*, November 6, 2018. https://www.curbed.com
/2018/11/6/18067326/boston-real-estate-cambridge-mit-biotech-kendall
-square.

Smart Growth America. "Dangerous by Design 2021." https://smartgrowthamerica
.org/dangerous-by-design/.

Smith, Neil. "Toward a Theory of Gentrification A Back to the City Movement
by Capital, not People." *Journal of the American Planning Association* 45, no. 4
(1979): 538–48. doi:10.1080/01944367908977002.

Speck, Jeff. *Walkable City: How Downtown Can Save America, One Step at a Time*.
New York: North Point Press, 2012.

Speck, Jeff. *Walkable City Rules: 101 Steps to Making Better Places*. Washington,
DC: Island Press, 2018.

Sunter, D. A., S. Castellanos, and D. M. Kammen. "Disparities in Rooftop
Photovoltaics Deployment in the United States by Race and Ethnicity." *Nature
Sustainability* 2 (2019): 71–76. https://doi.org/10.1038/s41893-018-0204-z.

Talking Cities with Matt Enstice. "Episode 18: Silicon Valley of Food Systems." February 21, 2017. http://talkingcities.libsyn.com/silicon-valley-of-food-systems.

Talking Cities with Matt Enstice. "Sewing Hope in the Lives of Others." June 13,
2017. https://talkingcities.libsyn.com/sewing-hope-in-the-lives-of-others.

Theodore Roosevelt Inaugural Site. "Olmsted's Pocket Parks of Allentown."
https://www.trsite.org/events/2016/08/06/olmsteds-pocket-parks-of-allen
town.

Thomas, G. Scott. "Business Next: Buffalo Is Now Second-Worst in the U.S.
for Child Poverty." *Buffalo Business First*, September 25, 2020. https://www
.bizjournals.com/buffalo/news/2020/09/25/buffalo-child-poverty-rate.html.

Tonar, Remington and Ellis Talton. "Cities Need to Rethink Micromobility to
Ensure It Works for All." *Forbes*, January 7, 2020. https://www.forbes.com

/sites/ellistalton/2020/01/07/cities-need-to-rethink-micromobility-to-ensure-it-works-for-all/.

Transportation Electrification Partnership, LACI. "Zero Emissions 2028 Roadmap." https://roadmap.laci.org/wp-content/uploads/2019/02/LACI-ROADMAP-V7-FINAL-HI-FI-1-020819.T6J-2.pdf.

U.S. Census Bureau. "Projecting Majority-Minority." https://www.census.gov/content/dam/Census/newsroom/releases/2015/cb15-tps16_graphic.pdf.

U.S. Government Accountability Office. "Investment Management: Key Practices Could Provide More Options for Federal Entities and Opportunities for Minority- and Women-Owned Asset Managers." GAO-17-726. September 13, 2017. https://www.gao.gov/products/GAO-17-726.

Wagner, Julie. "How Cleveland's Innovation District Is Advancing Equity through a New Kind of Anchor Institution." *Brookings*, November 9, 2020. https://www.brookings.edu/blog/the-avenue/2020/11/09/how-clevelands-innovation-district-is-advancing-equity-through-a-new-kind-of-anchor-institution/.

Wagner, Julie. "New Insights on How Innovation Districts Are Challenging Economic and Social Divides." The Global Institute on Innovation Districts, July 19, 2019. https://www.giid.org/how-innovation-districts-are-challenging-economic-and-social-divides/.

Wagner, Julie, Bruce Katz, and Thomas Osha. "The Evolution of Innovation Districts: The New Geography of Global Innovation." The Global Institute on Innovation Districts. https://www.giid.org/wp-content/uploads/2019/05/the-evolution-of-innovation-districts.pdf.

Watson, Donald, Alan Plattus, and Robert Shibley. *Time-Saver Standards for Urban Design*. New York: McGraw-Hill, 2003.

Yazel-Smith, Lisa, Andrew Merkley, Robin Danek, and Cynthia L. Stone. "Expanding the Indianapolis Cultural Trail: A Health Impact Assessment." *Chronicles of Health Impact Assessment* 3, no. 1 (2018).

About the Author

Credit: Paul Markow

Matt Enstice is the president and CEO of the Buffalo Niagara Medical Campus, Inc., located in Buffalo, New York. He started his career at *Saturday Night Live* working for Lorne Michaels. These days he is leading a pioneering, partner-driven initiative to integrate innovation, sustainability, health and well-being, and entrepreneurship to revitalize the city and the region.

Matt holds a B.A. in English from Hobart and William Smith Colleges and an MBA from Canisius College. He is a member of the Steering Committee for The Global Institute on Innovation Districts and serves on numerous boards, including the Buffalo Renaissance Foundation, the National Grid Advisory Board, Viridi Parente, Green Project Technologies, the Buffalo Niagara Partnership, Niagara University President's Council, and EforAll. Matt is also a member of the Alliance to Save Energy 50x50 Transportation Commission.

Matt lives in Buffalo with his family.

Learn more about the Buffalo Niagara Medical Campus at BNMC.org.